Inspirational Guidance Poems & Quotes

Empowering you through your awakening

04-10-2021

Disclaimer

This book intends to only offer information to readers for enlightenment & empowerment. It is sold with the understanding that the author is not liable for any physical, psychological, emotional, financial or commercial damages, including, but not limited to, special, incidental, consequential or other damages. If you use any of the information in this book for yourself, which is your constitutional right, the author assumes no responsibility for your actions.

Dedicated to all those who are seeking inspiration & empowerment.

CONTENTS

Introduction

Welcome,

 This book of inspirational guidance, poems and quotes has been written to offer support and guidance throughout and during your awakening.

 This is my second book which offers information and assistance in regards to the awakening process. The first book, "The New Earth Energy - Council of Twelve" which is a channelled book was published to share knowledge and guidance about the new earth and the whole process we are each going through individually and as a collective. It has a more in-depth explanation about the ascension process on a personal and global scale; it covers everything in more detail.

 You may wish to read that too if you haven't already as it will provide you with further information. It is not necessary though and you don't need to read that first before you read this book if you do not wish to. This book is more of a reference book offering assistance and insight while opening your mind as you awaken further to bring you more understanding and clarity daily about your life. Hopefully offer valuable insight on how to navigate some of the experiences you may encounter.

 I have divided this book into three parts for easier reading and so that it can also be used as a tool for offering you daily guidance and support if that is something you choose to do, it is entirely your choice. There is no right or wrong way to read this book. I believe that you will always receive the guidance you need in the right moment at the right time. If you are reading this book then it is no coincidence as I also believe that if you are you have been guided to do so.

 In the first section you will find a selection of inspirational writing in relation to the awakening process and some of the main aspects you will most likely encounter on your journey. Each one of you will experience life differently according to your programming, conditioning and belief system. It also offers further support in various aspects of life's issues and challenges you may be facing either daily or as a current theme which more often than not is being highlighted or playing out in your life consciously or subconsciously. Once you become aware of this then you can address these. Start to understand and then heal these aspects of you if you wish to.

The second part is a collection of poems that I have written over the past two years, many are based on my own personal experiences, thoughts and beliefs as my mind continued to expand and allow for further self-exploration during my own awakening process. I found that poems were a very easy way to express myself, my thoughts and my feelings which I knew many others were experiencing too. This was one way I could also offer support and advice to others who were also experiencing similar issues and could relate to my poems on a much deeper level.

The third section is a compilation of my own quotes which I found helpful in times of need to motivate me. Keeping me moving forward in my most difficult days and reminding me that life is just a journey that we are here to experience. That it is our emotions that play a significant part in how we interact with life. We get to choose whether we wish to react or respond to life. Once you become aware then there is no turning back.

So I invite you now to step a little closer and take a deeper look into your world and your reality. To think about who you believe you are at this moment and who you believe you are becoming. As you continue to awaken on your path releasing and letting go of anything that doesn't serve your highest good you will become more consciously aware of yourself as you connect with your heart consciousness. Your very own internal guidance system will assist you as you navigate your way through this journey called life.

Part One - Inspirational Guidance

Chapter One – Awakening

Are You Awake Yet?

Are you awake yet or do you choose to still live in your own little bubble? Repeating everything you do because it's safe and you believe that's what you are meant to do.

It's time to wake up and see the real world! Yes, there is more to life. Deep down you already know this. What you are seeing at this moment is a reflection of your own reality that you have created with your own beliefs. It's time to decide how you want to live your life. Clear the programming and conditioning which are keeping you trapped. Free your mind... Free yourself.

The Journey Called Life

I don't know about you but it has taken me quite some time to get to grips with the idea that life is just one never-ending journey with many ups and downs along the way. Always wondering why I am here and what is the point of all this anyway? This feeling of being stuck in the rat race trying to break free so that I can get to the finish line as if there is some goal to achieve or prize to collect at the end. Never really knowing if this is indeed true or just something we tell our self to keep going. Forever pushing forward not even stopping or paying attention to what is happening at this moment in time because somewhere deep down inside I have to believe the good stuff is coming soon and then I can have this amazing life that I keep dreaming about which everyone tells me is possible. So my question to you at this moment would be which fairytale do you believe? Cinderella...? Snow white...?

At the beginning of this great journey of life as a child, I was able to explore life and gain so much knowledge as I experienced things firsthand blindly believing that everything is true and never doubting, only asking question after question, following my curiosity about all things which happened to gain my attention. Storing everything I learned deep in my mind and belief system. I never really did understand why bad things happened or why things seemed so unfair while everyone else always seemed happy in life and appeared to have a better life than me or so I thought. Maybe one day I will be like them or better if I work hard and do everything right like I'm told, so I will try.

I have noticed time passes ever so quickly on this journey, minutes turn into hours, into days, into weeks, months, years and before I knew it I had experienced so much in my life, I would often think to myself, everything I choose seems so right for me. It's like everything in my life seems to unfold into the next chapter, flowing naturally from one stage to the next. I say flowing naturally as if everything is gentle but there are moments when lightning seems to strike and I'm riding the biggest wave of my life not knowing where it will end or where I will find myself. I hear a little voice inside my head saying okay stop this now...I don't like it...I want to get off. I realize that the voice I am now hearing is that part of me within trying to get my attention, the part of me that started on this journey with me in the beginning.

The wake-up call I needed to slow down and to pay attention to the journey, to put the brakes on, get off the motorway. So now I believe I have found my slip road which leads me onto the scenic route. I wonder how much more I will see now that I have slowed down. I wonder what I will experience next or whom I might meet on this journey called life? Maybe it will be you...

Life in the Fast Lane

Life is definitely becoming more interesting for me now since slowing down. I never really noticed how fast my life was actually going. Stuck on autopilot, living life I had been conditioned to live with what seemed like no alternative. I never stopped to even consider that there could actually be more to my life. That wasn't an option for me as I continued to be held in place by my early life conditioning and beliefs. My perception of life back then was much more limited, I listened to what others believed; believing I was keeping an open mind while deciding what was true for me. I started to struggle to understand how everything I thought I knew was now appearing to be so different in my reality. What was happening? I started to question my own sanity at one point. Is this real? Am I hearing things correctly? I found it more difficult to agree with the people around me who were once so familiar to me. How could this be? I was outgrowing everything I knew, not able to go back in time or stay in the life I had been accustomed to. My life was changing...I knew then it was time to move on.

Breaking Down

I was stuck in the box of limiting beliefs. I knew I had to break free... somewhere in my heart, I knew that there should be more to this life, this existence. I have experienced many setbacks in my life but managed to bounce back each time becoming the new improved version of me. Each time thinking yes this is it...This is who I actually am...While at the same time still trying to figure out how to move forward and to survive in this world. Stepping out leaving everything I know behind. These experiences were what I now considered to be only ripples in the water preparing me for the tidal wave yet to come. No one ever told me that there would be more than one box! That I would have many more struggles along the way. I do know that the first time I broke free was challenging. I didn't really understand what was happening to me. I was yet to find out.

What? There's more!

I always remember the first major awakening experience I had. It was like someone pulling open a pair of curtains to reveal the real world which had been hidden from me until that moment. Nothing I had ever experienced prepared me for the pure shock to my system as reality struck me deep down inside, not knowing if I wanted to laugh or cry as I tried to process this new belief which had just hit me like a lightning bolt out of the blue. How could this be? This is not true! That moment I knew my life would never be the same again. I was feeling so angry, feeling deceived by the world and now questioning all the conditioning and beliefs I had ever learned or been told. Then came the biggest question of all, who am I?

The Scenic Route

Approaching the exit...

I don't know about you but I have tried many times to get off this busy motorway of life onto the scenic route. Feeling excited as I approach the exit ahead, thinking it won't be long now until I finally leave this fast pace of life that I have so longed to escape, always knowing deep down that I have never belonged on the motorway. All I ever wanted was to experience life on the scenic route, believing it existed and desperately trying to find it. All the while dreaming of how wonderful my life is going to be, wondering what new opportunities await as I follow the open road ahead. Free to explore in whatever direction I wish to go.

New road layout ahead

At first, things appear different as I observe the new surroundings completely unaware that my ego is already in the process of reinventing itself, taking me on a little detour while planning to rejoin the motorway further down the road. Allowing me that short journey of freedom, giving me the feeling life is amazing, not having to navigate the busy flow of traffic anymore, carefree as I hit the open road having freedom now to choose a new direction. Although feeling a little apprehensive at first not having that familiar feeling of safety or boundaries that I had been used to I just knew things would be okay.

My intuition was becoming stronger as it assured me that everything was going to be fine. It wasn't long though before I had a feeling of fear rising up slowly inside me challenging my decision on leaving the motorway, telling me I needed to go back. It wasn't right to try and go out alone on the scenic route... It wasn't safe... I won't make it on my own, stop... go back before it is too late!

Oh No...Only a diversion

To my surprise it's not long before I find I'm back on route towards the motorway preparing to enter the beginning of the next experience life has to offer me as things start to speed up once more, again leaving me little option but to continue with the hustle and bustle of life.

Feeling trapped once more by the fast pace of life going down yet another motorway. It may look a little different but I know that it will soon begin to feel familiar to me again as I surrender to the flow and continue on the journey waiting for another opportune moment to leave again, still dreaming of what is to come while reflecting on where I have been. I remember how wonderful that brief moment felt as I found the scenic route. I now know it's real...I now know it does exist. Nothing is going to stop me now.

Finally

After travelling many miles, gaining much more confidence, learning how to navigate the busy flow of the motorway, becoming stronger I finally manage to silence the ego for a little while and delegated it to the back seat. My intuition now joins me once again as I slow down and leave the motorway, feeling more determined than I have ever felt before. The scenic route here I come.

Stepping Through the Door

How many times have you wondered about the real purpose of your life?

Have you ever noticed something seems to call you from deep within?

We all probably experience this at some point in our existence, opening that door! You know the one...it calls out to you quietly now and then. You know it's there and you say to yourself "one day I might just go and see..." Curiously wondering what will I find?

It may be just a quick peek at first until you gain the courage to investigate a little further. The only problem is though, that if you continue to do this then eventually you find that the door never seems to shut properly ever again! There seems to be a little crack appearing which you can just about see-through drawing your attention to it, calling out to you to take a step closer. Being as inquisitive as you are you decide to explore a little further becoming more and more intrigued at what you discover. Finding that life has much more to offer you than you could ever imagine, inviting you to step into the next room. If only you could be brave enough to explore.

The Choice

At this point, it still appears you have a choice and you probably do. Don't you? Maybe you can choose to stay where you are and pretend you didn't see anything. Forgetting this ever happened while trying to continue with your current life, accepting that this is all I know and it feels safe. You try reasoning with yourself, thinking maybe my life is a little stagnant at times but then life is supposed to be this way, isn't it?

"I don't get to choose what I want to do!"
"I have to just get on, as best as I can"
"It doesn't get better for people like me!"
"I should be grateful for what I have... At least I'm better off than most..."

Does any of this sound familiar to you? Ring any bells?

Now what you ask?

This is the choice many of you are facing at this time. Stay with the familiar life you know or feel the fear and venture off any way through the door into the new, into that room which calls you.

The only problem is you don't get given a guidebook or a set of instructions if and when you choose to step through the door. Once you make that choice there is no going back! You cross the point of no return. The only thing to do now is to find your way through the darkness. It's a one-way ticket, a journey of a lifetime. But somewhere deep down you feel it will all be worthwhile as you take that first step inside.

Trust in you...Keep the faith.
It's a personal experience from this point...

You become your own guide, trusting the process as all obstacles and challenges are confronted head-on whether you are prepared or not. It can be the most amazing experience or your worst nightmare!

9

This is all down to you, your beliefs and how deeply ingrained your previous conditioning and patterns are from your life experiences.

Onwards and upwards as they say!

Remain positive and accept all the help you can. You are never alone...Ask and it is given.

You may find as you are making your way through the darkness help and assistance may seem to appear out of nowhere along the way. You may even find that after a while you can assist others as you join together in sharing your knowledge and experiences you have discovered so far and the journey continues.

Always remember...If in doubt, surrender to the process. Remain positive and know better is yet to come. Finally, you are searching for the truth within. Your biggest question of all...Who am I?

Does Your Logical Mind Appear Broken?

Are you confused?

Funny, how we always believe our most logical thoughts lead us forward on our path to the right place, right time or right thing we need in our life. We never question this as it has always served us well until now. We trust it... We see it... It is right! ...But... Now you may be finding that this doesn't appear to work in the way it did before. "There's something wrong" you might say! What's happening? Things are going wrong. I followed all the rules and did everything I am supposed to do but it doesn't work anymore. What's happening? The more you try to fix it or try to review things the worse it seems to get. "I don't understand," you say and maybe seek help or advice from others. Sometimes this proves helpful for a short time but eventually, you find that all aspects of your life seem to be changing and feel out of control. Your logical mind doesn't work the way it should, so what now? Where do I go from here?

Feeling Stuck?

When do we accept that our life is not working the way it is supposed to?

You probably start by asking your most trusted friends and family members first if they have experienced anything like this and how did they fix it? This is okay in the beginning, but eventually, you will probably find that many of them will eventually look at you strangely and think you are having a moment... A mini-crisis...A meltdown...Or whatever else you wish to call it. They don't get you! Any more...You've changed! You don't fit in with them which may make you feel lost.

Maybe...It isn't you that is having "a moment" but someone close to you and you feel stuck in the middle... "How do I help them?" you say. What do I do? Everything I have tried doesn't fix it... I don't know what to do! I don't like this! I want everything to go back to normal!

You may also find that you withdraw from everyone and say nothing. You smile and carry on with your life pretending to the outside world that everything is fine, while inside your screaming out for help, putting on a brave face, hoping your mask doesn't slip.

At what point do we own up to our truth?

All of this is okay for a while but eventually, you will find your outside world comes crashing down around you and shakes you to your core, this you cannot ignore anymore. It's time to face your truth. It's time to ask "what is really happening?" It's time to own up to your own truth.

What will people think about me?

You will feel the fear as you imagine how people will react to you. You may feel really uncomfortable with the thoughts that now come to the surface as you start to imagine the reaction of the outside world judging you. Your mind becomes full of thoughts that seem to spiral out of control. You may even question your sanity as you now know and become to realise you are not the same person you thought you were and now people are actually telling you this. You imagine the

11

worst and possibly feel isolated, alone or trapped. How do I get people to like me again? How do I gain acceptance from everyone? I want to fit in with everyone and feel part of everything again. These are only fears, they aren't real. Once you recognise this you will find the chatter in your head will eventually become quiet. This is just your ego.

Why do people treat me like this?

You begin to question how people react towards you.

Why are people so cruel? Why do they hurt me like this? Why have they changed their behaviour towards me? And it continues, you may protest your innocence at this point and say "I have done nothing wrong!" You may try to plead with them hoping they will accept you...BUT THEY DON'T...Finally, the doors close and you feel all alone.

Congratulations...You have now realized that you cannot fix yourself from the outside.

The solution you seek can only be found within...

Awakening...Breaking Free

Exciting times are coming

For those of you that don't know we are going through an awakening process.

This information has been known for some time now so that we could prepare the way for many to transition into the new earth. I am being guided now to share my own journey and to provide help and support to those of you who need it. It is time for me to now step out of the closet! (The spiritual closet) just in case you're wondering...for those of you that know me I have already come out of that closet! For those that I don't know, I mean (The sexuality closet) So many labels.

It has been a very challenging life for me at times and I have known for quite some time now that I have chosen to be of service in this lifetime. I have already experienced many obstacles and challenges in my life to prepare me for the work I am here to do. Finally, I am now ready to begin my work of service and share the information I receive with you. I do hope that the information helps you in some way to prepare you for your awakening process, especially if you are just now beginning to wake up. For those that are already in the awakening process, at whatever stage you are at, then hopefully you may find some of this information helpful or just comforting knowing that you are not alone on your journey.

What's happening?

Many of you are aware that things seem to be different in your life at present. At times you may be feeling a little lost or confused and have no explanation why you feel like you do. Some of you are already going through the awakening process while many are still sleeping and have no idea of what is about to happen to them. There are of course some that have chosen not to go through this process in this lifetime, if this is your choice then you will finish out your life and transition as you normally would. We have all be given the choice, there is no one being left behind.

Although there are some people who have already started transitioning through this process believe that everyone is now awake, I do not believe this to be so. This is the reason why I am being guided to share this information with you. I myself did believe at one point during my own transition which started in 2006 that by now, everyone should be at the same level as me, that no one would need this information. I now know that through my own experiences this is not so.

I would also like to share with you that I believe I am still going through this awakening process as there are many stages to it. I have come to the conclusion at this time that there appears to be no end once it has begun and that we will always be learning and evolving during our life here on earth. I also believe that it would not be possible to go through this process more quickly or all in one go, as a human being we are not capable of this. I would say upon my experience it appears that I was being spoon-fed information slowly,

13

allowing for the new changes to take place gradually, so that they made sense to me and I could accept them and integrate them into my belief system.

I would like to take this opportunity to say that the information I share here is only intended to give you some insight and understanding of the process you may be going through. This does not replace any medical care or any medication you are currently receiving.

Why it's happening

Although there has been much information available to everyone in regards to the ascension process for quite a few years now and what it involves for the people on earth, many of you have not taken it upon yourselves to gain access to this information for one reason or another. I do not intend to give a full explanation about the ascension process here as this is not the only purpose of this book.

We are all going through an awakening process and becoming aware of who we really are. We have all chosen to be here at this exciting time to be part of this great transition into the new earth. Even if you don't agree with this information at this moment, eventually you will come to realise this is the truth.

The Awakening Process

This will be different for each and every one of you as it will depend on what needs to be released from your conditioning and belief system. You will go through many changes within all aspects of your physical, emotional, mental and spiritual well being. There is no time limit to this process and there are no targets to reach. It is simply a process to clear and remove anything that no longer serves your highest good.

The Purpose

It is to allow you to live your life as you choose without being conditioned or controlled by others. We are to be free to experience life as we wish. Everything, as we know it now, will continue to break down and new systems and structures will be put in place. We are being allowed to start again and live as we were always intended to live.

To be free!

Help... I think I'm Going through the Awakening Process

Many of you at this time in your current state of awareness may be questioning your purpose for being here in this lifetime. You may be beginning to search for answers outside of yourself, seeking information or advice from others who appear to be more knowledgeable than you at this present time or who can at least give you an explanation of where you are at in your current state of mind or how to help you navigate the current issues or crisis which appears to be unfolding in your life. You know you are feeling different and are not quite sure what is happening to you. You may feel confused and find your life seems to be literally falling apart.

Each and every one of you is all at your own stage of the awakening process. Some of you are only now just at the beginning stages while others of you are further on in the process and may have experienced more than one awakening experience already. These people may seem more advanced than you who are only now awakening for the first time but this is not entirely true. There is no right or wrong time to be going through this process. It is always at the right time for you when you are ready.

What is the Awakening Process?

There are many stages to the process but some of you are led to believe that it is all designed to follow a certain pattern or that there are certain steps to completing the awakening process. This again is not entirely true. There are no set rules or procedures to this process, it is an individual experience. There is no right or wrong way to go through this awakening and there is no set length of time for any stage to be completed. It is true to say though that once this process commences then there is no going back. You cannot return to your previous state of being asleep. Each and every one of you on earth at this time has chosen to be here to go through this experience. It is not happening by accident or coincidence, everything that is happening to you during your experience here at this time has already been planned by you.

You will always follow your own unique path and the steps or stages will be different for each and every one of you. This is because you have all be subjected to different experiences and conditioning during your life. This has become hardwired into your belief system which you currently believe to be your reality.

The whole awakening process is purely to expand your consciousness from your limiting beliefs and to prepare your physical body for the ascension process in which you will be ascending from the 3rd dimension to the 5th dimension of reality.

There is much information already available about the process of awakening and ascension but as more and more of you are now finally awakening things have continued to progress and evolve since this information was first made known. So the people who may have already completed this process and previously shared their information in regards to their own awakening of what they experienced may not always be the same for you and what you will experience now. Things have progressed and become much easier now as the pathway has been forged by the first volunteers.

There are some similarities you may experience with others in regards to the physical symptoms you may experience within your physical body and there are also some similarities within the mental and emotional processes too. These can be experienced during different times throughout your awakening process and can be more or less severe depending on what you need to release and clear within your own belief system, previous conditioning, physical, mental, emotional and spiritual bodies.

The First Stage of Awakening

The first stage that many will experience will most likely be in regards to the mental faculties. This can usually start as a major life event or experience which is usually traumatic. Many believe that this experience is their actual awakening and that from then on even though they recognize the changes within their thoughts and beliefs as they are being challenged they also think that this is it. They are now fully awake to life and that life will now just continue for them in a new way. They have no idea that this is only just the beginning of their awakening process and there are more stages to experience in the future. They all serve a different purpose and they will all be experienced differently.

The first awakening is usually the most shocking and life-changing to you. This first stage can take the longest to process as this is where you need to adjust to being more consciously aware of your reality. This is where you challenge your thoughts and beliefs and gradually adjust to your newly discovered reality as you revaluate your belief system. You start to notice how much you are now changing as you are becoming aware of the previous conditioning and beliefs you once believed as your truth.

You may seek out more information and guidance at this time and want to research as much as you can about the many spiritual aspects of life and other existences within this reality. You will want to gain as much knowledge as you can. This is when you can be easily influenced or manipulated by others and easily led to follow others who wish to take advantage of you. Some people are not who they say they are and will try to take advantage of you when you are vulnerable and open to be misguided.

It is important at this time to remain open to the information without judgment as much as you can. Use your discernment and only follow your inner guidance as you adapt to your new reality. You may come across all kinds of information that may cause you to fear or doubt yourself. You may feel that you need to seek out further help or guidance from others at this time. Always follow your intuition if you choose to do this and only take what information resonates with you as your truth.

You will find that as you gain more knowledge and information your belief system will continually change as you try to find what resonates with you as your new reality. This is likely to change as you progress through this process. You will continue to grow and adapt to what feels right for you. Please do not worry if you find yourself being challenged or others question you as they notice the changes within you and your personality. You will find that you will no longer fit in with the people around you. Everything in your life will now be changing as you are changing your beliefs and perception. This is a necessary process that may feel uncomfortable as you go through it. It is best to try to go with the flow during this stage. If you try to fight or resist this process it will only become more difficult for you and delay your progress. Eventually, things will become stable again in your life as you settle into your new beliefs and reality as they become more accepted and balanced.

Chapter Two – Inner You

It's Okay to Be You!

How many of you feel that you are not good enough?

How many of you compare yourself to others?

How many of you make judgments about yourself or others?

Do you realise that these thoughts are all learned patterns of behaviour?

We are all guilty of thinking like this at some time in our life. We don't seem to be able to control these thoughts. Our thoughts are like continuous cycles that are stuck on repeat. We create our thoughts out of habit. Sometimes we may create our thoughts to protect us, for our own self-preservation, especially if we feel threatened. Sometimes we believe that comparing ourselves with others helps us feel better, even if it is just in that moment.

Did you know...?

The first time you recognize yourself becoming aware of your thoughts, actually thinking this, may come as a shock to you? If you just stop now for a moment, think about your last thought. Do you remember what it was? Would you consider it to be a good thought? Was it positive, negative or neutral? Would you like to change that thought now you have reflected on it? Well done...If you do...You should be pleased with yourself if you catch yourself thinking this way.

Why may you ask?

This is the first step to recognizing your thoughts, knowing you are aware of your thoughts is the breakthrough you need to start to help yourself in changing how you think. Once you recognize your thoughts, you can then start to recognize the patterns within your own thinking process and choose if you still want to continue with your current thought or replace it with something better. The choice is yours; with practice, it's possible to change your thought patterns.

Once you begin this process you may find yourself noticing when you are thinking something negative or something positive. You then can choose to replace it if you so wish.

Do you know your thoughts create your reality?

You do get to choose your thoughts, each and every one of them and once you are aware of this then you can create whatever you desire.

So what do you really think about yourself?
Do you think it's okay to be you?

The choice is yours to make. In the meantime I just wanted you to know "It's okay to be you!" You are good enough. You don't need to compare yourself to anyone. You are already perfect. You just need to recognise this for yourself.

Accept All Aspects of You

Do you accept all aspects of yourself, or do you try to ignore or hide some of them?

When you become aware of your unconscious programmes and conditioning that are playing out in your life and you are finally ready to accept that they are aspects of you. Then you are ready to begin the healing process fully integrating them within your whole being.

We often project these aspects of ourselves outwards unconsciously onto other people and blame them for the things we are experiencing, not taking any responsibility for them. It takes time to accept these parts of yourself and integrate them fully but once you do your life will begin to transform. You may be surprised at what has been unconsciously playing out in your life when you start to become aware of these hidden aspects.

Things that can help you

Take all the time you need to do your inner work. You may find it a really difficult process to go through at times, just know that everything will be okay. There is no right or wrong way to go through this integration process. It is different for everyone. Trust your inner guidance as you become more aware and always loving and gentle to yourself. Pay attention to your triggers, this is usually highlighting some aspect of you that you need to accept and work on. Most importantly accept every part of you. Rejecting any part of yourself will slow the process, cause you more pain and keep you stuck.

Sometimes in Life Being an Empath.

Sometimes in life, I find it hard to speak. I don't always know what to say. Sometimes in life, I feel a little sad and often just want to cry. Sometimes though, I'm full of joy, laughing and joking or even singing a song. Sometimes I never know how to feel, I can get confused about what's real. Is this me I am feeling now? It's hard when you're an empath, especially in a crowd. It can get so confusing with everybody's thoughts, when you soak them all up, just like a sponge. Thinking you're crazy or losing your mind, as you hear all the chatter going around and around in your head.

But after a while, you come to learn, how to discern what is yours, and what is not! You may be so sensitive that you just start to cry, as you hear a sad story from someone passing by. You can get so emotional with the slightest little thing or even quite hysterical and laugh at everything. But after a while you accept this gift within, you find yourself more compassionate for everyone you meet. You've learned how to become detached, you've learned to become more discreet. You still pick up on every little thing from the people that you meet as you go about your day, but now you have learned to put your barriers up, so it doesn't affect you in the same way.

Empaths – You and Your Energy Field

As an empath, it's very important to clear your energy every day. It is so easy to forget. Especially when you're busy schedule demands your attention. So if you're feeling overwhelmed or more tired than usual, perhaps you are carrying more than your own energy and it's a sign to clear yourself. We can often forget this simple thing that we need to do every day. We sometimes don't notice until it gets to the point of feeling really out of sorts. A quick simple exercise you can do every day is to clear your energy while you are bathing. Make it part of your daily routine. Notice how different you feel! As you do this more often you will recognize much sooner when you're picking up from others. Get to know how your own energy feels. Then you will be aware if you start to soak up other energies around you.

Empaths - Understanding Your Energy

Top tips to understanding you & your energy

I found spending some time in my own surroundings helped me. I also found it helpful to just sit with my own feelings and emotions. Just by observing all of my own thoughts and feelings and recognising how I felt helped me become more aware of myself. Clearing my emotions and thoughts rather than trying to stuff them back down inside helped me to respond more in the now moment. Once I had learned to process everything at the moment as it came into my awareness I became more able to experience my feelings more naturally. This was the most important thing I found I needed to do. It's important to get to know yourself like your own best friend.

The next three tips may take some time to get to grips with, be patient as you practice these.

- You need to discover what your energy feels like.
- You need to understand your own feelings.
- You need to get to know your own thoughts.

These three things are important. They will help you to recognise how you really feel. When you are picking up anything from others or your surroundings, you will then notice a change or a shift in your energy, your thoughts or your feelings. If you know how you are currently feeling, and then you suddenly feel different, it's most likely not you or your energy.

It is very important to establish good boundaries for yourself. This will help you to decide what is acceptable to you. It will let others know too, where they stand with you. You can visualize yourself surrounded by a bubble of white light which will protect your energy. You can do this daily if you choose to, especially before going out into busy environments.

More importantly, if you feel overwhelmed at any time, then take time out and clear your energy field. Check-in with yourself often. Eventually, it will become second nature if you incorporate this into your life as a daily routine. If you absorb too much outside energy within your body all at once thinking they are yours, then you may become more emotional or tired than you normally feel. You may even feel aches and pains within your physical body which are not actually yours. It is important to clear yourself often if you notice any of these changes within you and you know they are not yours. You can simply say "what is not mine please leave" This is a simple technique that can be used whenever you feel the need. It can be said in your head as a thought and it will still be as effective if you are conscious about speaking out loud or if it is not appropriate for you to do so at the time.

Advantages

Finally, on a more positive note...

When you have practised becoming more aware of how to discern your energy from others long enough, you will find being an empath has its advantages. You will be more prepared for assessing your surroundings and the company you keep with others. You will notice how others are feeling and how they are really responding towards you. You will be more aware of how you feel in certain situations and surroundings giving you more options on what you wish to experience and what you don't. Life will become easier to handle and you will be

23

able to intuitively avoid people or situations more quickly before they become an issue for you.

Empaths - Clearing Your Energy

Here are some top tips on protecting your energy that I believe will be beneficial to you.

The most important thing you must do is to shield yourself & your energy. This stops you from absorbing everything like a sponge. (Especially, if you are feeling confused, tired or depressed). You can do this by visualizing a bubble of white light around you. This can be done at any time & can be implemented daily, ideally when you wake up. When you shower visualizes your body being cleansed of all the unwanted energy. This will help to clear your energy field. Alternatively, salt baths are also great for cleansing your body.

Carry crystals that offer protection.

They ideally need to be carried on your person. (I wear mine in my bra) I would recommend labradorite. Bronzite is an excellent crystal for further protection, especially if you are in a negative environment, as it will also return the negative energies to the sender. If you want a crystal to absorb negative energies, then either black tourmaline or black obsidian is ideal, or a more gentle crystal to use would be snowflake obsidian. Remember to cleanse your crystals often as they too need to be cleared of the energy they absorb.

Finally, another tool to use when you feel you have absorbed external energies or feel negative thoughts from another is to declare that "anything which is not yours, please leave!" you can also add "and be returned to the sender" if you wish. I usually ask that it is returned to source. (I would recommend you say this in your head as you may attract some further attention)

If you do happen to think of something negative yourself & feel you realise this, then simply say the word "Cancel" as soon as you can or even during the thought. This then cancels the thought & also helps you to retrain your thinking as you become more aware of your thoughts.

Intuition

Do you sometimes find random thoughts popping into your mind, sometimes they may seem strange and you don't always understand?

Do you find your head sometimes feels like it's spinning in circles, going round and round as if it's in a loop, repeating thoughts throughout your day, not making sense in any way? There is no logic to the thoughts you have so you question your sanity as you think you may be going mad.

You may sometimes get the most amazing ideas or little flashes of insight into the solutions you seek. They seem to pop up out of nowhere when you least expect them to even sometimes when you're trying to sleep.

Do you ever have a thought of your friend you haven't seen in some time? You can see an image of them pop into your mind. Not long after they usually get in touch, just to say hello or to offer a helping hand. Isn't it amazing how they always seem to connect with you at the right time for you! Funny it seems like they even knew.

These are signs of your own intuition. Helping you and guiding your way. The more you pay attention and listen to them the stronger and more accurate they will become. It's usually that first fleeting thought or feeling you have at the moment that is true. But if you try to make sense of it or think too long your ego will try to take over and confuse you.

So if you have random thoughts popping into your head. Just ask yourself what does this mean to me? Then wait for the answer and always trust your gut. It's your inner guidance just getting in touch. It's always been there inside of you waiting for you to notice when you take the time to connect. So just quiet your mind and you will be amazed at the answers you find.

They will mean so much more to you, than asking someone else what they would do. The answers are there whenever you ask. Always remember it's your higher self otherwise known as the more intelligent part of you.

Synchronicities

As you notice the synchronistic signs throughout your day and smile. Have you ever thought are the signs there because you are consciously manifesting your desires and they are reminding you that you are coming into alignment with them? Or are they there just because it is what you are unconsciously thinking about in your life? I wonder.

Synchronicities (Signs) many of you are probably already aware of synchronicities, especially if you have already started the awakening process, but for those of you that aren't, I thought I would share some of my personal experiences of synchronicities and how they first started to give me guidance in my life.

So what are synchronicities?

Firstly though, it is important to know what they are as this will give you some idea of what to look out for as you go about your day. They can be signs, symbols, pictures or sounds you see or hear which seem to make an impression on you, especially when they are repeated at different times, places or situations within your life. At first, you may just notice random things popping up that stick out to you or get your attention. Most people call these coincidences. People tend not to pay much attention to them and dismiss them as soon as they appear. Not thinking anything more about them.

Pay Attention

If you do begin to pay attention though, then they will show up more and more. They are part of your internal guidance system playing out in the physical world. The more you pay attention, the more they will continue. Some synchronicities can be a part of your internal guidance. These are usually things like songs playing out in your head. Words that seem to pop into your mind randomly, that are not related to your current thoughts.

Have you ever heard people talk about seeing signs?

I never really understood what people meant when they talked about seeing signs. I didn't know what they were talking about. I realised though that I had actually been experiencing synchronicities but not actually knowing what they were called.

For me, my first experiences I remember started back in the beginning stages of awakening. I remember seeing the word "meditation" everywhere... It repeatedly appeared to me in various ways, news articles...television...books...magazines...and I even recall hearing it in conversation when talking to people.

I remember being told that if I wanted validation about something then if I received outside validation via three different sources it was usually a sign and confirmation telling me it is the right thing for me to do.

I remember also at times that I didn't always understand the synchronicities I was receiving as they sometimes came in a way that needed to be interpreted by my own internal guidance system. Symbols are used very often as signs and we need to be able to decipher them to gain insight from them. This takes practice so don't worry if you do not understand these straight away. It took me quite some time to work these out, frustrating at times as they continued to appear more and more until I worked it out. You will find when you have understood the message then it will not repeat anymore. This is a sure way to know you have received the information and understood the message it was giving you.

Do you hear songs?

I hear songs in my head; they can play out at various times. I don't tend to get the same song unless it is related to a certain situation or person. Sometimes they may just be random songs but what is important about them are the actual words or the song itself as they are trying to convey a message to you about a certain issue or problem you may have or as confirmation about a certain situation or person you are enquiring about.

Some songs do repeat again to me at the strangest of times. I can wake up during the night and have a song playing out in my head. It has driven me mad at times as I know the song but not all of the words. The only way to get it to stop sometimes is to search for the song on the internet. Listen to it, work out the meaning then acknowledge the message.

Numbers

There are many of you seeing numbers. This again usually happens when you begin the awakening process. They can be random numbers or in a sequence. The most common numbers people mostly see are 11.11. These were the first numbers I recall seeing. I see numbers everywhere! Clocks... internet...signs...television...number plates on vehicles. They constantly show up in my life everywhere. They all have significant meaning to me and it took me a long time to understand that these are a way to activate certain information within my conscious mind which is related to my awakening process.

Words

These too can appear anywhere and repeat over and over again. I find repeating words usually give me confirmation of the answer to my current question I have. This too can now pop up as a thought in my head or a sign outside as I'm going about my day.

Things to remember...

Pay Attention

Signs will come to you in your own unique way. They are personal to you and only you will know the true meaning. The more you acknowledge them, the more they will appear to you. They are there to guide you. They will help you to choose the right options for you. Learn to interpret them in your own way. They are only meaningful to you. Signs can be anything that gives you insight, guidance or solutions.

Inner Work

When you find you keep attracting the same circumstances in life and you begin to notice a pattern or theme playing out and question the reason why then you are ready to begin your inner work to address the real core issue or wound which is held deep within you. If you want real change in your life then it is your responsibility to do the inner work needed to clear these. There are no quick fixes, yes it might be painful to accept your inner wounds but once you address these and clear them you will be glad you did.

Free yourself, be kind, be caring and remember to accept and love every part of you.

Be Mindful of Your Thoughts

Be mindful of your thoughts. Your thoughts create your reality. Do you like what you are creating? It's never too late to change your focus. Just you changing your thoughts will eventually change your situation or reality. Your feelings add to getting what you desire. So be mindful of how you are feeling. Emotions will steer you in the right direction. Positive thoughts are best. Negative thoughts will cause resistance and slow down your desires. You are a very powerful creator. Everything you desire starts within you.

Are You Aware of Your Thoughts?

The most useful word you can use while you're trying to reprogramme your conscious mind is "cancel".

When you observe yourself repeating negative thoughts during your day, just say the word cancel as soon as you become aware. You will eventually become more consciously aware of your thoughts if you do this. This is also a good practice when you have already spoken out loud. It is not too late to immediately say "cancel" if you are aware of what you have just said and no longer mean it. (You may want to say this in your head only if you are in company) Practice this every day. It is simple yet so effective.

Emotions

Become aware of your own emotions. When you can observe just how you feel. See how you can change in just a moment. As everything you see, always seems real. Your reality is of your own making. It's what you believe to be true. Your emotions help you to understand the flow deep inside of you. Like a ripple in the water, or the trickle in a stream. Sometimes like a tsunami, completely overwhelming you.

When you can acknowledge how you feel, no matter the situation you are in. Own all the feelings you have inside, sometimes it's just an adrenaline rush, maybe anger, happiness or joy. Even just the reaction to our flight or fight response. They all serve a purpose in our life when we learn to use them correctly in times of strife.

But the trouble with how we live today is that we have all become desensitized to the normal way. Our emotions don't respond in the way they should. Instead, we're all numb with no feelings at all. Sometimes this is making us completely withdrawn.

So it's back to basics to learn how you feel, in all your situations you experience in life. Reset your system allowing you to respond correctly, to your life in an appropriate way. Instead of being triggered throughout the day, or not even responding at all, not even aware of your emotions any more.

But if you take the time to learn how you really feel, expressing all your emotions once more as they are meant to be. Life will have so much more meaning for you in everything you feel.

Reset Your Emotions

Every day when we wake up we start the day completely reset. When we sleep we automatically clear our emotions and return to a neutral state. So when you awake feeling refreshed before you decide to recall everything before you going to sleep ask yourself this. Do I wish to continue with the same thoughts and emotions today? Or do I wish to start feeling new? You decide... It is your choice, but whatever you choose enjoy your day.

Chapter Three – Projected Reality

Expectations

What expectations do you have in life?
Do you set your targets way too high?
Or is it what others expect from you? That causes all your
problems in life for you.

Expectations can be hard to achieve when there are no limits or targets to reach. People keep expecting more and more which is never-ending, it just seems so unfair.

They don't even care how hard you try, they just say that's not good enough and find fault every time. To them, the expectation is just like perfection you might as well forget it and not give them your attention.

The best thing for you is to release and let go. Just remember to do your very best, put in the effort and never give up. This is the most important thing for you to do. Then you can achieve great things and smile.

Happy you no longer need these people in your life, with all their expectations they dictated to you, telling you you're not good enough, that it will never do. Walk away and listen no more, just set your own goals, be positive and remember that you can achieve so much more.

Do You Ever Question Your Reality?

Do you compare your life to others or try to control everything?

We never really know how our life will unfold. We all have dreams and desires in life but sometimes life doesn't happen the way we imagine it to be. But whatever does happen always seems to make perfect sense upon reflection, and you see that what you experience in life all connects together like a long thread as each event or experience leads into the next.

So if you ever find yourself trying to control the outcome of your life or a certain situation and you meet resistance along the way. Instead of trying to keep knocking on a closed door, perhaps it might be time to let go and allow things to unfold naturally as they are meant to.

The Cycle of Life

Sometimes In Life...There will be times when you wish to remain silent and withdrawn from the world. This is a time to reflect, to process all that you have achieved so far on this journey. To release anything that no longer serves you. To prepare for a new chapter or stage which, will be beginning shortly in your life. If allowed, life flows naturally in a cycle. Life only becomes a struggle when we try to change the process, hold onto things that we have outgrown or we try to block our progress forward when we fear change.

Just like a butterfly, there are processes to life. Sometimes the easiest thing we could do to progress forward in life becomes the most hardest to do, as we become attached emotionally to everything around us. This is the time to pause, allow yourself time to adjust to your current situation and most of all be kind and caring to yourself. Eventually, you will find you will move forward again at the right time as you allow yourself to just be in the moment and go with the flow.

Practice Being Consciously Aware

As you go about your day begin practising being consciously aware of all that you experience. Whatever experiences or challenges you may be facing today. Try to stay consciously aware as much as you can. Think about how you feel in each moment. Notice how this may change as you interact within different situations throughout your day. Notice how you engage with people and what effect they may have on you and how you feel about it.

When you become more aware of yourself more consciously, notice how it may even change how you see the experience, challenge or situation, you are experiencing. Just by being consciously aware in each moment noticing how you interact with everything can change your perception. You may even decide to engage in a completely different way or even find a solution to your most recent challenges. If you find you get caught up in any drama. Don't feel bad about it; just bring your focus back to yourself being consciously aware again. The more you practice this, the easier it will become. Until eventually, you will find you experience life in a whole new way.

Eventually, you will be able to maintain a more conscious state of mind for longer periods of time and begin to notice how you engage with everything around you at the moment. You will be able to choose how you wish to interact with others and be aware of the dramas which are currently playing out in your life or the dramas which people are currently playing out around you. By being consciously aware you can remove yourself from any situation or drama which may not be in your best interests without having to make such an issue about it. You can just simply step out or disengage at any time you choose. You will also be able to intuitively know what is most likely going to happen as you become more aligned with your own reality. Living in the now, being consciously aware, allows you to fully engage in the experience more fully.

How many times do you go through the motion of doing something on autopilot not even paying attention to what you are doing or even being aware of the experience you are having? Imagine that whatever you wish to experience now in your life can be like a brand new experience as if you are experiencing it for the very first time. Wouldn't that be a great place to start?

Drama

How often do you get caught up in drama? Do you ever stop and think why?

Did you create it? Or are you taking on someone else's drama?

Are you going to keep repeating the same drama over and over or are you going to detach yourself and do something more deserving of your time? Haven't you got anything else better to do?

It's your choice.

Don't waste your energy on things that are not important. Make your effort count for something meaningful to you. The change starts with you.

De-clutter Your Life

Do you de-clutter all areas of your life?

When we clear out anything from ourselves, our home or our surroundings we create space. This then allows for new to come in. Everything is energy. You need to keep it flowing. Make time to de-clutter today. You will be so glad you did. You will feel lighter.

You may find it too much of a challenge for you in the beginning so start small. Choose just one thing to clear, then another. Before long you will find it an easy process to do. Never hold on to things out of guilt or because you think you might need it. Let energy flow.

Do You Know Someone

You probably all know someone in your life who wants you to do all the hard work. To find out all the secrets to having a happy successful life, and then inform them for free so they don't need to make the effort and put in the hard work.

Unfortunately for them!

It's an inside job so they will most likely remain stuck if they choose not to do the work themselves.

Fortunately for you!

If you are doing the inner work needed to progress in your life, you will receive the rewards for your hard work. By doing the inner work, eventually, the person, who tries to take advantage, will understand what is happening and either get on board, or they will eventually not resonate with you anymore and naturally leave your life.

Letting Go

Letting go of all the conditioning, patterns, programmes and learned behaviour allows you to fully engage in life. To create and experience love, joy, happiness and freedom as you are meant to.

Go within... Take back your power, your freedom, your choices and your life.

Release and Let Go

When you release the past...
Letting go of things, that no longer serves you.
You create space to allow the universe to bring you.

- New experiences
- New opportunities
- New love

What do you desire?

Choose to release and let go. Step into your new life. It's waiting for you.

See Beyond the Illusion

The truth is you're never stuck. You can choose to free yourself whenever you want. You create your reality. You believe your drama but do you realise you are not your story. You are a divine being having a human experience. See beyond the illusion! Set yourself free.

Trying to Control the Outcome

When you try to control the outcome of your current situation or desire in life you are limiting your possibilities. You are also creating resistance. Let go of trying to control the outcome. Surrender; accept that everything is being worked out for your highest good. Allow the universe to bring you what you need. You may even be surprised that you receive something better than you wanted. Trust the process; go with the natural flow of life.

Chapter Four – Shadow

Feeling in the Dark

If you are in the dark feeling lost.
Thinking life is against you.
Remember...
Try to remain positive.
Stay strong.
There will be light again.
It's just a process you're going through.

The Shadow Self

There seem to be so many struggles in life regarding the shadow self. People are actually living in fear and believing that the darkness and evil are going to hurt them!

What you believe to be your truth will be.

You create your beliefs with what you observe in your surroundings. We attract to us everything in life consciously or unconsciously.

Be aware of your thoughts. If you believe in evil and watch horror movies then your mind will most likely create more of this in your reality. If you believe in conspiracy theories about the world, then this too is what you will see more of. When deep-seated trauma comes up to be released it can take form in many ways depending on what you believe.

So my advice to you today is when you are challenged with the shadows of life. Stand strong and face them as the darkness will continue to feed off your fear. You need to know that you are fully protected always and nothing can harm you unless you give your consent and power to it. Trust your own inner guidance and if something does not feel right to you then pay attention!

What you will eventually discover is that all your beliefs are being challenged. You are going through an awakening process and are no longer accepting other people's truths as your own or the previous patterns and conditioning you have accepted as your truth. You are creating a new belief system that will go through many changes as you challenge everything within your own reality. It is up to you what you choose to believe in. It is also important to know at this point that as you expand your consciousness and your perception changes so too will your beliefs, so you may find that you seem to contradict yourself as you are continually changing your beliefs.

Allow the process to flow naturally

The more you allow the process to flow naturally the easier it will be. When we get in our own way and cling on to our past beliefs or refuse to change then we create more inner conflict. We tend to look to others for advice and support when we feel stuck or have conflicting views which is okay but always ask yourself if this is your truth too. If it does not feel right within then question what is true to you. Do not follow blindly just because you feel lost and trust others to have the answers you seek. Always go within, if the answers do not come straight away trust that they will when you are ready to receive them. Sometimes we may feel blocked or delayed on our path which can happen to you many times. Know this too is part of the process to allow you time to fully process the changes you are experiencing. Do not think you need to try to fix you! You are not broken! You are where you are meant to be at the right time on your own path. Your experience is unique to you. You are being re-birthed into a new version of yourself as your old outworn beliefs and conditioning are being cleared away.

What I know to be true within my own experience

We must accept every possibility can exist! Question everything you see, hear or feel in your reality. You may be shown things which you never thought possible, or you may even now discover what you previously believed was true is not anymore to you. But it does not say we need to believe in all things as our truth. What you believe to be your truth will be. You create your beliefs by your thoughts which then manifest into what you observe, hear or feel within your surroundings. We actually attract to us everything in life consciously or unconsciously.

Do not try to fix you!
You are not broken!

It's time to remember you have everything you need inside of you already to create your best life yet.

Do not let the outside influences or distractions prevent you from being who you are meant to be. Choose you! Follow your heart, let it lead the way. It's okay to be you! You are being re-birthed into a new version of you.

Vulnerability

Do you ever consider yourself to be vulnerable at any time?

Do you see being vulnerable as a sign of weakness or as a strength?

Often in life when you feel vulnerable you may want to put up protection to keep yourself safe from harm.

That can sometimes be beneficial to you but when does it start to become an issue?

It is not always to your benefit to put up protection as it also stops everything else from getting through your barriers. You can be so busy putting up your walls to keep yourself safe but by doing so it also prevents all others or things from getting through. To me, being vulnerable is a sign of strength.

It takes courage to let down your defences or take down your walls, allowing you to expose yourself to all feelings and emotions. Practising being vulnerable more often will allow you to experience life to the full. You will still be able to protect yourself if necessary and choose when to put in your boundaries, instead of having them permanently in place.

Think about where you may feel vulnerable in your life or have you so many barriers in place you may be blocking everything from getting through?

Is it time to allow you to be more vulnerable?

You may find it difficult at first to allow yourself to feel vulnerable and expose yourself to feelings and emotions you are not able to process very easily, but keep trying. Sometimes the fear of being hurt can prevent you from being open to receiving love, even though deep down you know that is what you truly desire.

Keep going... Be Strong... Be Vulnerable...

Free yourself, be kind, be caring and remember to accept and love every part of you.

Consider Your Baggage

Have you ever considered how much baggage you carry around with you?

I don't mean physical baggage. I mean all your thoughts, beliefs, hurts, anger that you may feel. This too is all baggage. Just because you don't see it with your physical eyes doesn't mean it's not there.

Imagine if you could physically see this stuff. Do you think you would still be holding onto it?

Be kind to you. Check-in with yourself. Take a good honest look at the things you choose to keep hold of. Then ask yourself one simple question.

Why?

Choose today to let go of all the things that no longer serve you. To let go of things that keep you stuck. Let it go and be free.

Surrender

When you come to realise that your beliefs and conditioning are the real cause of your drama and pain.

Just stop...Surrender...

When you realise that trying to control everything and everyone to make your life better doesn't work.

Just stop...Surrender...

You see, you don't need to fix anything! You don't need to control anything! You can choose to just stop anytime you want. You can choose to be free from drama anytime you want.

Find the path of least resistance. You will be glad when you do. The drama will keep you stuck. Trying to control your life will keep you stuck.

Find your flow... Allow everything to just be.

Let go...Surrender...Just be you... What leaves your life let it leave. What no longer serves you release it. What you enjoy do more of.

Remember you choose!

Inner Wounds

We all reach a time in our life when we finally stop trying to be good enough. When we stop trying to fit in as we never seem to win no matter how much we do.

When you finally realize it's not your fight and you don't need to accept the things others project onto you. The feelings deep down inside you've been trying to hide are preventing you from actually being you. You have carried them for so long, believing you are always wrong as you feel the wounds deep within.

But now you see you can no longer hide from being the real you. You no longer accept what you're being told as you know it's just not your truth. Your eyes are now open wide as you discover the truth; it is not what you are led to believe.

You recognise your self-worth and you choose to be free from the things that have held you back. You have finally found your voice from within and become the very person you were always destined to be. As you step into your power and finally speak your truth. You finally heal the wounds that have prevented you from being you.

Do You Believe You Are in Control of Your Life?

When you finally stop trying to control everything, life becomes so much easier. The only thing you need to do is just let go, let your life flow naturally. The most important thing in your life is you! Bring your focus back to you. Your power lies within. Stop trying to control everything outside of you. When you create from within, your outer world will eventually reflect this back to you. Take back your life, take back your power. Go within, follow your own guidance. Allow life to just be, but most of all love you.

Feeling Confused

Whenever you feel confused in life, slow down! Get out of your head. Do something physical to ground your energy.

The answers you seek will show up in your life when you need them. Not when you want them to by trying to control the outcome. Trust your inner knowing, not your mind. Your mind is programmed. It will keep you going round and round in a loop keeping you confused.

The answers you seek come from your inner knowing. Trust the process, be patient. All will be known in the right moment, stay in the now. The past has gone; the future is not yet created.

Just allow the journey to unfold and go with the flow.

Interaction

When you become aware that everyone you interact with in your life is here to help you progress on your path, remember to give thanks to them for being part of your experience.

Even the most difficult interactions you have to help you to grow, to become stronger. To help you discover self-love, to increase your self-worth. To help you become the best version of yourself. Without them, we could never have these experiences.

Time-Out

If you ever feel upset, emotional, angry or overwhelmed while engaged in a discussion or conversation with another.

Just remember...

It's okay to take a step back! Disengage from the situation.
Take time to review your situation or circumstances you find yourself in. Never feel the need to give an instant response just to please someone else.

Likewise, if you find it is the other person who is reacting towards you! Don't respond or react. Don't get sucked into their drama. Walk away. If you do decide to interact then only choose to do so when they are calm.

When a person is angry, emotional or upset, they will not retain anything that you say to them. So do yourself a favour! Don't waste your time.

Chapter Five – Transformation

Fitting In

When you try to fit in with everyone else but you know deep down that is not who you truly are be honest with yourself, do what is right for you. Break Free, it may feel wrong at first. You may even question yourself or even feel guilty for not following the crowd. This feeling is only temporary.

Stay strong! Listen to your own inner guidance. It's okay to be different. It's okay to be you!

Fix You

We all reach a time in our life when we get to the point of total surrender. This usually comes after we have tried to fix ourselves many times over without lasting results. We are led to believe parts of ourselves are broken or we are not good enough as we compare ourselves to others. Nothing we do seem to fix this.

We try everything we can to create a better life but seem to make little or no progress. Our problems never get solved; quick fixes soon fall apart as we listen to advice from friends & family or maybe seek professional help which still leaves us feeling like we have failed in life. No one understands you completely or has the solutions you seek.

The truth is no one has the answers for you! Yes, you can have great support, a great network of friends and family or any other number of support systems but the truth is they are not able to fix you. Because the real truth is you are not broken! When you're ready to accept this then you will stop searching outside yourself for answers on how to be you, spending all your time procrastinating trying to assist everyone else while ignoring your own life.

Do you know everything you are and need is inside of you? We hold this truth and knowledge within but we are taught to seek everything outside of us. This only prevents us from connecting to our inner knowing and power. It is time to seek your answers within. Listen to your inner knowing. Follow your own guidance. Allow all of your limiting beliefs to be stripped away. To discover who you truly are and not what you have been told to be or believe.

Take back your power, go within, and connect to you, your inner knowing and your guidance. Find your truth then realise you can choose to be your true self.

Trust the Process

When you learn to trust the process of life and allow things to come to you in divine timing you begin to live life in the now. Know that whatever is meant for you will not pass you by. Not all opportunities are right for you. Learn to listen to your inner guidance this will help you to decide. Ask yourself the question is it yes or no. Then wait for the answer. It will be there if you slow down and pay attention. You will know if and when it's time to take action.

Learn to trust your inner guidance. Sometimes in life, we just need to wait. But we are programmed to be constantly busy, always in a rush. We believe it has to all be done now! Doing things we don't want to do instead of just saying no. Bring your awareness back to you. Slow down, enjoy each moment, allow and be in the now!

Excuses...Excuses...Really

How many times do you hear excuses from your friends or people you know in your life? Sorry! I haven't been in touch with you lately but I've been really busy! We must catch up soon! I will call you! Hopefully...You get the point!

But if you are becoming aware of this then you are probably asking yourself what have I done wrong? You haven't done anything wrong. You are finally beginning to see the truth.

You know yourself if you want to commit to someone or something, then you find the time regardless of what else is going on in your life. If it's important and means something to you then you make the effort...right! So take a look at the people who are currently in your life.

Who makes the continued effort & find the time for you?

Hopefully, you consider them genuine.

But what about the people who are not?

The one-way friendships! The friends, who expect all of your time, but have no time for you! The friends who keep you around to make them feel good! The friends who continue to create drama, keeping you trapped in their world, which just use you for their own personal gain.

So, now you are starting to see the truth. But you try to make things right and continue to make the effort. Stop feeling guilty, you don't owe anybody, anything! It's okay to let go of these people and their drama from your life. If you feel you are not able to as they are significant people in your life that's okay. You can still choose to put yourself first. Love and respect yourself enough to know you deserve better because you do.

It's okay to choose you. Put yourself first! You will be so glad when you do. The more you change you will find these people will change too. Some will even automatically leave your life as you will not resonate with them anymore. The good news is that this will allow space for new friendships in your life, more aligned with who you truly are. Now isn't that worth knowing?

Do You Ever Come First

Do you ever come first?
Do you respect yourself enough to put your needs first?
If you don't, ask yourself why?

Sometimes you may have a valid reason not to, but often it is a sign of codependency.

Always love yourself first.
Always take care of your needs first.
Always make sure you are happy first.
Always respect yourself enough to say no if you choose to.

It's not being selfish
It's being kind and respectful to you.
If others don't like it
Then that's their problem, not yours.

Spiritual Law of Responsibility

Do you ever actually wonder what your responsibility in life is?

In life, we are asked to respond appropriately to any situation. It is our own personal responsibility to prove we can handle all situations responsibly with honesty and integrity.

Each person is responsible for their own wellbeing and destiny. We do not have the right to carry someone else's burdens for them as this would inhibit their personal growth and deny them their responsibilities.

When we take responsibility for someone else's choices and decisions we do not serve their highest good or spiritual growth. Our responsibility is to strengthen and empower others and encourage them to carry their own responsibilities.

We project our own judgments and feelings onto others. When we don't speak or act from a place of honesty about a situation, or how we feel about someone or something out of fear, anger or jealousy we are creating an injustice to both our self and the other person or situation. So when we do speak honestly we release ourselves from the situation as well as the other person.

When we truly understand what responsibility is to us we no longer need to blame others or project our judgements and feelings onto others any longer. So taking responsibility isn't about what actually happens but how you react.

As you go about your day perhaps give some thought about what you consider are your responsibilities in regards to the people you interact with within your life and where you might be projecting your judgements or beliefs onto others.

Do you try to take control of other peoples issues or problems as though they are your own and do you decide you know what is best for them regardless of what they want?

How many times do you take responsibility for others?
Are you aware of your own judgements and feelings you project onto others?

Now knowing this, how will you choose to react in future?

Limiting Beliefs

Do you still hold onto limiting beliefs? Are you comfortable in your daily routine unable to accept change?
Does everyone else seem to change around you while you stay the same?
Do you know that making gradual changes in your life can help you on your way to start changing your perception?

Changing your perception opens you up to a whole new level of reality. The more receptive you become the greater your consciousness can expand allowing for more positive flow into your life. Start today, make that change. Any change is good! Be a rebel and try something new. You never know, you just might like it!

What Label do you choose?

It causes so much confusion when you're trying to find your identity in this world. Trying to fit in, using labels just wanting everyone to accept you as you are. Labelling yourself so you belong somewhere! When you choose to be free you realise you don't need labels. You realise that it's okay just to be you.

Judgement

It is difficult not to judge another especially when you are conditioned to. I know I still sometimes catch myself judging someone for what they may have said or done in the heat of the moment. Especially if it is something that still triggers me. But I'm more aware of my actions now and try to think before I speak.

I try to accept where I'm at in my awakening process and don't beat myself up if I slip up. I know I'm only human and I'm still releasing and clearing my programming and conditioning. I don't honestly know if I will ever be completely free from that as our minds are designed to be programmed. But I can be aware of what I allow myself to be exposed to. I can still have a bad experience! I just don't let it be my main focus if I feel I have done something wrong. I try to put it behind me and move forward.

The other thing I know I do more of now is to just observe life without judgement. I just see things for what they are, accepting what is. I see how things came to be. I am able to see the root cause of an issue or situation. I see the blocks people have or where they are stuck. I respect where people are at in their life. I know they are where they are meant to be. I know everything just is... what it is.

Mind Daily Workout

Have you ever considered that your mind needs a daily workout just like your body? We spend so much time on our physical appearance and how we look to others but we need our mind to be clear and alert. Become aware of what you are absorbing with your mind. Look for the positive in all you do. Train your mind to think positively. Then see your world transform. Remember to think positive. Be positive and smile.

Mirror

When you look in the mirror what do you see? Do you see just your reflection looking back at you? Or do you see so much more?
Do you see love, do you see beauty, do you see perfection or do you only see all the things you wish to hide? All the aspects of your body you have tried to deny? Do you believe that beauty is only skin deep? Do you compare yourself to others, wishing you were like them? Do you avoid the mirror completely so you don't have to look at yourself?

I know when I look in the mirror...I am happy to see the real me. It has taken some time to accept all of me as I learned to love myself. Self-love is the kindest thing we can do for ourselves.

How Flexible Are You?

When it comes to change how flexible are you? Are you someone who makes a plan and decides things have got to be a certain way? Or are you able to adapt to change?

When we are able to allow things to flow naturally throughout our life without it having to be only one way, we find the experience is much easier to deal with.

It only becomes more challenging when you become rigid in your way of thinking or doing. Then things start to become more difficult and you find them harder to control or navigate through.

Try to be more flexible when you are next challenged in life. Find alternative solutions if you can. Sometimes though, when you allow things to unfold naturally, they tend to sort themselves out.

How many times have you spent all day trying to sort something out only to then find it all somehow gets resolved in the end by some other kind of intervention? Isn't that amazing!

Don't be so quick to fix everything. All you really do then is waste precious time and energy on something you have no control over.
So remember...Flexible is best.

Advice or Not

When you find you need advice or support in life...You can choose.

When people want to give you advice on your life because they say they want to help you. Sometimes this advice lands on deaf ears and doesn't resonate with you. It will only make sense when the time is right for you so you can learn what you need to. Then you can move forward on your path when you are ready to continue to experience what you have come here to experience in this life. People may try to fix you along the way, or tell you how they did it their way. But that may still not be right for you. It just causes friction between you and the other person as they try to convince you that their way is best, that you don't need to invest in anything else than their advice that they are giving you as they are right. They tell themselves that they are the only ones who can help you.

Do you need advice about your business?

Then some people will tell you that they have the solutions you seek for your business. They will promise to help boost your business and provide you with follow up leads. Provide you with an amazing service and increase your sales and your client base. But all they want to do is to earn money from misleading you. They are not interested in the services you provide within your business or what it is you do. They will try to sell you more of their services by using promises to boost your business, to help you gain more leads with the information they provide and they will try to get you on board, at the beginning with a free webinar, a special offer or a free trial.

They will try to hook you in with all the promises they make, convincing you that if you invest your money with them they will guarantee to increase your sales. They prey on you when you're at your most vulnerable knowing they will convince you in the end with increased pressure to invest in their amazing products by emphasizing that they are only available for a limited time. They tell you they are different and not like the rest. But it's not too long until you start to see the truth of who they are and how they are trying to manipulate you into purchasing their services.

They too are human just like you and me, but their ego has usually taken over at this point and they are too blind to see how it is in charge of them. Their intentions are not so pure after all. You're just another business transaction to these people now trying to make more money no matter how they present themselves. They're convinced that is what's most important in life, material gains and a larger net worth. If you pay attention you will notice how they always emphasize how much money they are making...how many clients they have and how busy they are...how they have spent all this time perfecting their skills and knowledge and they are now giving you all of this for free...to help you to be successful just like them...Really?

That may be true for a few genuine people out there but before you consider investing your time and money with any of these people use your discernment. Ask yourself if it is the right thing for you? Never feel pressurized into anything. We are all here to experience life. Have you ever considered that the way you are doing things in your business is meant to be part of your experience? You are having your own unique experience and gaining valuable insight and gaining knowledge along the way. Nothing is guaranteed in life for anyone. Not even the most successful person in a business can guarantee your success.

Use your judgment when you need advice

Use your judgment when you need advice, your intuition will guide you and keep you right. Find the people that you are drawn to the most, that way you will know they are the right people to help and guide you in your time of need. You will know who they are as they will be pure of heart and want to support you from the start without a hidden agenda or doing it for personal gain. They will be honest, sincere and true, wanting to help you, believing in you or what you have to offer. If you are ever in doubt then take a step back and wait to see how things unfold in your life. You will be shown the right way forward when the time is right for you. Never give your power away to anyone else. You can choose what is right for you! Remember, it's your life, your journey, trust the process.

What Are You Good At?

How many times do you fail to notice how much you have to offer the world? (Probably...every day)

Do you compare yourself to others, or think they are better than you? (Probably...every day)
Do you know? We all do that! We are all conditioned by limiting beliefs. It is learned behaviour.

Unfortunately, we have all been conditioned in life to compare ourselves to others. We automatically believe we are no good at something even before we know for sure. How many times have you stopped yourself from experiencing something in life out of fear or just because you believe you will fail if you try, so you believe it is better to accept your failure now to save you the embarrassment of failure in the future? You put limits on yourself, thinking you are protecting yourself, but you are doing yourself an injustice by allowing false beliefs to dictate your life experiences.

Just for today only think about what makes you, you! We all have our own unique skills and talents, things we enjoy. Instead of limiting yourself by focusing on the things you believe you are no good at trying to concentrate on the things you know you are! Look for the positive things about you. It's so easy to put yourself down and focus on what you can't do, all this does is make you feel bad and creates more negativity.

Just by becoming more aware of being focused on the positive things you will automatically start to change your perception and help you to begin to feel more empowered and in control of your life.

In reality, you can do or achieve anything you choose. It is only your beliefs that limit what you think. Just imagine if we all did the same things in life, it would be pretty boring, don't you think?

Never be afraid to try something new, have a go. Sometimes it's more fun trying something you know you may not be the best at, but at least you can say you made the effort.

You never know, you may even find something you're naturally good at.

Now wouldn't that be something!

Chapter Six – Empowering You

No Limits

There are no limitations in life; you have everything available to you. It is your perception and beliefs that places a limit on everything. You miss the opportunities because you are not open to see them. It is time to expand your consciousness to open your mind to all possibilities.

Always remember, if you think it, if you believe it, if you know, it if you see it. Then it is possible!

Do you remember?

Life is perfect, everything is fine. Do you remember you are divine? You're exactly where you are meant to be on your current path of your reality. Piecing, the entire puzzle together, present, future and past. You realise it's a perfect game which you have chosen to play. Finding your way out of this MATRIX is your priority of the day. As you awaken more and more integrating your, higher self. Remembering the most important thing is to love you first.

How to Be Successful

I Know I'm probably not the only person who is constantly being bombarded every day by adverts & people telling you how to become successful, how to succeed in life, with their amazing online programmes, which you should watch and sign up to, so you too can be successful now.

Give me your money and I will share my secrets with you! Blah, blah, blah... While they put you down, pointing out your current failures and how you are doing it all wrong!

Well after much thought. I still come up with the same answer I always did. Hopefully, you will too!

How many times people have tried to tell me I'm not good enough, I will never be successful and I will fail.

Sounding familiar to you?

I believe we are here to experience life. We have already decided our path before we incarnated. Why do we need to follow others and pay them money to learn whatever they did on their path? Why is everyone still promoting how to be successful by how much money you make or how many followers, leads or clients you have?

Surely your path is unique to you!

You may have chosen to experience many different scenarios about setting up a business and what it means to you to be successful. Does it mean if your business is not the same as everyone else's then you're a failure? I think not!

Follow your own path! Do it your way! Part of the process is having fun and engaging in the experience. Not the end result! So before you keep chopping and changing your mind about what you are currently doing in life, because others keep telling you it will never work or be successful.

Ask yourself this...

- What is right for me?
- Do I need help or support right now?
- Do I need to make changes in what I am currently doing?

If you are like most people here at this time then you are here to introduce new systems and structures, then why would you model yourself from something that is already in existence?

Follow your own inner guidance. Trust in your path and be conscious not to get sucked back into the system.

Be you! Do it your way. After all, that is what you came here to do!

Living in the Moment

Living in the moment allows you to fully engage in life. There is no need to look back to the past. The past has gone. The future does not exist. You create your future by what you do in each & every moment. Surrender, to the now. Choose to live in the now. Say yes to life, change what you can, and accept what is. Everything is working out in your life perfectly. After all, you chose this life. Relax & let life unfold, enjoy the journey.

Manifestation

When you get so excited by something you've manifested. You see it in your physical reality and you're so pleased with yourself. Just remember to remain focused. Don't let it distract your attention from your inner world back out into your outer world. Your power always lies within.

Me Time

When you take time out to have some "me time". You get to find out how wonderful you are. You get to experience the things you like to do. You get to appreciate what makes you happy. Too much of your time is spent giving in to others wants needs and demands, also known as people-pleasing. So today choose to please you, get to spend time with you. After all, you spend your whole life with you. So doesn't it make sense to get to know who you are? It's a positive start to loving yourself first!

Slow Down and Enjoy Life

When we take the time to slow down in life we get to see things more clearly. We get to see the things we usually miss in our everyday reality. We notice the things we usually take for granted. We see things we have never seen before. We get to observe life in a more meaningful way. We get to enjoy the experiences we have on a deeper level. We get to appreciate friends and family. We become calmer and in control of our life. We make more conscious choices that are better for us. Life becomes so much more when you choose to slow down. Try it, live your best life now.

Remain in the Moment

When we remain in the now moment we get to appreciate everything as it is. We get to experience life as it is meant to be. We can enjoy and appreciate every aspect as it unfolds. If we pay attention we get to notice even more. Just by slowing down and observing life, we can have a completely different experience. You get to choose how you experience life.

I wonder what you will choose today.
I wonder what memories you will create today.
Make them count.

The Natural Flow

Do you ever find that you seem to achieve more when you don't plan your day?

I find if I try to follow a list of things to do it takes me longer and some things don't get done. But if I just go with the flow I seem to complete things more quickly and fit even more things into my day.

How about you?
Have you noticed this?

Inspire

We all need a person in life we can inspire to be like. We all need realistic goals we can achieve. We all need to feel loved. We all need to acknowledge our talents and gifts. So remember if you need these things in life, then so do others. Remember to acknowledge other peoples talents and gifts. Offer praise and encouragement where it is due. Give thanks and gratitude for all that you have. Treat others as you would like to be treated yourself. Respect where others are at in their life. Always, lead by example, walk your talk and speak your truth.

Your Fairytale

Imagine…If you were to write your fairytale what character would you be? Have you ever thought that the character you choose is probably already who you are inside? You already have all of these qualities within you.

Happiness

Live your life the way you want to. Do the things that make you happy! We spend too much time trying to figure things out in our life instead of just being happy living in the now. Don't be afraid to be who you are! Or do the things you love. Start every day with the intention to be happy. Do something you love every day. Break your goals down into small steps that way you get to appreciate the small victories on the way. Always remember to keep your focus on the prize. Know that you are a winner.

Chapter Seven – Awareness

Authentic Self

Don't you find being yourself is so easy?

It only becomes hard when you try to be someone else.
Follow your own path.
Do what makes you happy.
Follow your own authentic life.

A Positive Mind

A positive mind creates positive thoughts. Positive thoughts raise your vibration. Your vibration attracts the things you are in alignment with. So remember...To create the life you want, all you need to do is be positive.

Actions Speak Louder Than Words

Sometimes in life, there is nothing you need to say.

Actions speak louder than words.

When you finally come to realise in life actions do speak louder than words. You get to notice who are really there for you in life. You see people for who they really are.

Do you like what you see?

Be Yourself

Do you find being yourself is so easy? It only becomes hard when you try to be someone else. Follow your own path. Do what makes you happy. Follow your own truth. Live your own authentic life.

Face Your Fears

When you finally decide to face your fears to take the plunge and make that change. You finally build up the courage to let go and surrender, as you jump off the cliff and then you realise... There is no bottom!

Manifesting

When you get so excited by something you have manifested. You see it in your physical reality and you're so pleased with yourself. Just remember to remain focused. Don't let it distract your attention from your inner world back out into your outer world. Your power lies within.

Give Thanks

Whatever you experience in life remember to give thanks and gratitude.

We all learn by our experiences even though some may be considered negative or more challenging. There is always something positive to be gained through every experience even though you may not think so at the time.

As we are not always aware of whatever our life has in store for us on our journey then the easiest path to take is the one of least resistance. We do this by living in the now. Not in the past as this has gone and not in the future as this does not yet exist. The power we have is in the now. This is where we experience life in the moment. This is when we can choose how to respond to life. So remember, choose wisely. Give thanks for the experience and give gratitude for all you have.

Keep Moving Forward

Keep moving forward in your life even though there may be times when you're having so much fun. You just want to stay in the moment and experience it forever. But situations always change. They are meant to keep flowing. Remember to keep moving forward. Never try to hold on to anything. If it is meant to stay in your life it will. Enjoy every moment living in the now.

Your Path

How many times do you wonder in life if you're on the right path?

Has it ever occurred to you that you're on your path!

It only becomes confusing when you try to walk someone else's.

Sometimes in Life

Sometimes, in life, there is nothing you need to do. We are led to believe we should always be busy doing, but sometimes all we need to do is just be still. Allow the universe to work for you. Learn to be patient. Be kind to you. Allow the process to unfold naturally in the right moment when you are ready.

In the meantime relax... Go with the flow.

You will know when it is time to take action and move forward again.

Opportunities

Life is full of opportunities, do you see them?

There are no limitations in life; we have everything available to us. It is our perception and beliefs that place limits on everything. We miss the opportunities because we are not open to see them. It is time to expand your consciousness. Open your mind to all possibilities. Always remember if you think it, if you believe it if you know it and if you see it then it is possible.

Life Purpose

Are you trying to find your life purpose?
Do you wonder what it is you're supposed to be doing in this life?

Like most people, I often wondered that same thing.

Do you hope someone will tell you what it is or how you can find out by following someone else?

Firstly stop trying to work it out. Your purpose will show up for you when you are ready. The best thing you can do in the meantime is to live your life how you want to. Do the things that make you happy.

Your life purpose will be something that makes you happy so chances are if you continue to do what you love then you're going in the right direction!

We spend too much time trying to figure things out instead of just being who we are and doing what we love. Start today by being happy doing what you enjoy. Everything you need for your purpose is already inside of you. No one else can tell you your purpose. Just be you and it will show up and reveal itself when you are ready.

How Amazing Life is When

How amazing life is when you start to see the bigger picture. You can see the truth in all realities. That everything is right, that everything just is.

Have you ever defended your truth to the point when your truth was the only truth, that all other truths were wrong?

I guess that caused some arguments and conflict for sure.

Did you ever stop to consider that the other person or their point of view was also right?

We only see life from our perspective most of the time. But if you allow your perception to expand and accept that there is more than one truth eventually you will find that this is true.

Yes, people project onto you at times but that is a whole different discussion.

My point I'm trying to highlight here is your perception will change if you accept that there are limitless truths and possibilities.
Try it... Next time you have a different truth, belief or opinion from another; try to see it from their point of view. You may learn something new. Keep an open mind. Acceptance is the key, you may not agree but you can try to understand.

Victories

Life becomes amazing when you can appreciate all the small victories you achieve each day. When you can smile to yourself knowing you have created everything you intended to do just the way you wanted to. By taking small steps each day on your path is sometimes all you need to do to manifest your dreams. Eventually, your dreams become your reality. Remember if you can think it. You can create it.

Part Two - Poems

An Angel by Your Side

As you wander through your life. You may come across some trouble and strife. Along the way when times get tough, you are on your knees, you have just had enough. You are not made for this you say, you have reached your limit, you cannot take it anymore. As you begin to cry as you fall to the floor.

You continue to pray, asking for guidance from above, you feel abandoned and all alone. Still, you keep struggling, praying while feeling all hope has gone. Trying to stay strong, wondering where I went wrong. Asking God and your guides please help me.

In your hour of need as you continue to plead, thinking that they must not be true, as they do not seem to answer you. When out of the blue, when you are most lost and you are through, you begin to feel a presence beside you, a loving feeling appears deep inside, and you just know everything will be fine.

I am an angel you hear and we will always be near, we will always walk by your side. We are always here. Please have no fear, as we watch over you all of the time.

We protect you from harm, we have been with you since you were born, supporting you in every way. You only need to ask for our love and advice then acknowledge the signs that we send you. This could be a feather, a coin, a song that you hear, or even the smell of sweet perfume.

You will know we are here when we are near as you will feel our love in your heart. We want you to know that we are all one. Part of the loving divine, we will help guide you and continue to protect you until the end of time.

A Loving Heart

My heart chakra is now activated and I feel so alive. I feel all the love filling me up deep down inside. The love just keeps on growing as it expands far and wide. Touching everyone I meet as I walk throughout this land. The love I feel is like I have never known before. It's like love has taken on a completely brand new form. It means so many things to me now as it grows more and more. It makes me feel alive as it continues to explore.

I'm here to share my love with you all, each and every day. Hopefully, you will embrace this love as you feel it connect to your heart. This is the gift I bring to the world so you can feel this love too. For love is a very powerful thing, it's what will one day set you free.

We are all slowly remembering who we are and what we came here to do. To remember we are divine and that love will guide us through. As we come together as one, standing side by side, we all intuitively know our hearts will eventually unite.

A Precious Gift

Sometimes in life, there are no words to say, just how you feel. Sometimes in life, you just need a hug, as everything seems surreal. We don't always know what to do, or how to show our love. Even when we are absent from you, it doesn't mean we don't care.

We feel so deeply within our hearts of all the pain that others share. Trying to stay strong, supporting our loved ones as you strengthen the love that is already there, uniting the bond deep within our soul, showing them that we are there. That each day we have is a precious gift that we should treasure and keep forever more.

For nothing is ever promised in this life, so live every moment without fear. Speak your truth often with kindness and share your love each day. One day will come and they will be gone and you will still have so much to say. We cannot turn the clock back or live in the past and the future has not yet arrived. So live in the moment and express all you can, even if it is without words.

A Rose

Love can be just a pure as a rose. To be admired for the love it represents. Its beauty compared to your love, deep within your own heart. So delicate, yet sensual, its petals as pure as silk, as you reach out, to feel its soft touch, always be mindful as you get closer as it protects itself with its thorns.

Are You Ever Triggered?

When you're triggered and you're really mad. You're angry and you're losing your rag. You don't know what to say. You just rant on in such a way. That nothing you say makes sense. You stand your ground protesting your innocence. Pointing your finger at everyone saying it's their fault why things are wrong.

"It has nothing to do with me," you say when the other person tries to walk away. "I'm just the victim, can't you see, why are you always having a go at me?" "It's not my fault, you're to blame, and you have always been the same". "You make me angry and make me shout until I forget what I'm annoyed about".

It's just a vicious circle that keeps going around and around. The ego just loves it as it makes you feel so proud. You never really actually see the wound that's inside of you, which is the real reason why it triggered you. So if you take the time to reflect and address your wound within. You will find in time your trigger is healed, never to react again.

Remember to thank the person who helped to trigger you as without their help you would never have known, this wound inside of you. So if you find you are ever triggered again, I'm sure you will do your best. Not to go off little a bottle of pop but to stop and smile, do your inner work and then take some time to reflect.

Be Happy

When you wake up in the morning before your start your day, imagine all the happiness you will get to create today. No matter what you do or where you go, remember to take your happiness with you.

Spreading your happiness as you go, watch how other people start to show their happiness too as they interact with you. Real happiness is a feeling that is created from within, not from an attachment from outside of you.

When you discover happiness from inside your heart, it won't be a conditional thing. It will be a constant part of you and your life, it is part of that loving feeling you cannot hide.

When you find your happiness it will be here to stay, there is no going back to sadness or any more gloomy days. It's time to leave all that behind now as you know what real happiness is, it's time to shine, to be the real you and live from your happiness that you create from within you.

Believe in You

There may be times in your life when things seem uncertain, or you have worries and strife. You seek the answers outside of yourself. Feeling confused not knowing what is right.

You may wonder what to do; the answer is so simple when eventually it comes to you. You will realise you knew all along, when you trust, have faith and believe in you.

When you seek the answers outside of yourself, you give away your own power and confidence. Trusting someone else may have the answers for you, especially if they don't actually know you, will only cause you to delay, creating more confusion along the way.

How can someone tell you what to do, who has no knowledge or history of you? They have never walked by your side or even a day in your shoes. But still, they try to give you their advice and tell you what to do.

They don't know your master plan or what your soul has chosen to do. The life you decided to experience was chosen especially by you. So isn't it now obvious, that the answers you seek are all inside of you?

So if you feel you are ever stuck or even feel like you are in a rut. Take your own advice never think twice, listen to your intuition, and let it guide you. Never doubt yourself again always believe in you.

Be Who You Are

All the love and beauty you hold inside, is just bursting out to be shared far and wide. It's time to show the world who you truly are. Shine your light like a guiding star. The children need you now to show them the way. To be strong, loving and supporting in each and every way. They are our future of this new world, which we are all creating if the truth is told. Open your hearts and let us all now see. Singing and dancing, feeling happy and free. Together we are all creating life's tapestry.

Be Your Authentic Self

Live your life the way you want to. Do the things that make you happy! We spend too much time trying to figure things out in our life. Instead of just being happy living in the now. Don't be afraid to be who you are! Or do the things you love. Start every day with the intention to be happy. Do something you love every day. Break your goals down into small steps. That way you get to appreciate the small victories on the way. Always remember... Keep your focus on the prize. Know that you are a winner!

Bipolar...Mental Health...Society Today

When you keep everything inside, and never speak about how you feel. To the outside world, you may look fine; people never see how your feelings are affecting you.

You go about your day wearing a mask, pretending all is well so they will never ask. How are you they may say? And you reply everything is okay! But what you want to say, is no I'm not...really okay. I'm finding it hard to cope today. I don't know what to do, to cheer myself up as I feel so blue.

It's hard to be happy all of the time when your moods are unbalanced and you feel them decline. Some days I'm bouncing off the walls, feeling so hyper I can't sit still. I just keep going on and on, like a fully charged battery that can last for days. Other days I find I'm not so good and just stay in bed under the covers as each day passes until I recover.

It's hard to find a balance so I fit in, I just want to be normal and feel happy within. I can't remember the last time I felt normal, but as I compare myself to everyone else, I know I'm not the same!

Some people judge me for the way I behave. They have no idea of the daily battle I face. But I would love to tell the world this is who I am. I am doing my best to live my life the only way I can.

I don't want medication to block out who I am, or have a man in a white coat telling me how to live. Putting me in somewhere safe, telling me it's for my own protection. The world is not equipped to deal with people just like me, so they stick a label on what I've got and blamed it on society.

They say it's all about the trauma you have suffered as a child. You will never be the same again it has definitely ruined your life. They never really address the real root cause. They just treat the symptoms by drugging you up with pills. The pharmaceutical company wins in the end, making even more money. They keep you in the cycle as it's all just about supply and demand.

They may increase your dosage every once in a while or offer you a new pill and say it's a new trial, as your body becomes more tolerant each day, you never even consider they are bad for your health. You believe the doctor is taking good care of you, but they are just as much to blame and they know it's true. They know the tablets you take are doing more harm than good. The medication will never fix you and they know it never could. It's now time to wake up to the truth, to finally take back your power. After all, it is your life and you should choose how you want to live.

Broken

You're not broken you're just you! You're only different because of what you have been through. When you think you're broken and you want someone to fix you. You've seen so many specialists who have given advice to you. Nothing seemed to make a difference no matter how you tried. But did you know there is nothing wrong with you? They just took your money and lied.

You just need to clear your mind. It's the programming that keeps you stuck. It repeats the pattern making you continue the cycle again. So you continue to seek out guidance which confuses you all the more.

So now you know you're not broken and there's nothing to fix in you. You only need to process and release all the trauma you have been through. Your brain shuts down to help you cope when times are difficult for you. This is to allow you to regain your strength and to acknowledge what you're going through.

You will release and let go when the time is right and you're guided to do so. You're higher self will always protect you no matter what you believe you are going through. Everything happens for a reason even though it may not always be clear. But clarity will come to your mind when the time is right for you, to gain insight and understanding of why and what happened to you.

You are meant to be who you are. Your experiences are chosen by you. As you continue on your path your intuition and your guides will always support you. The guidance always comes from within, you only need to ask. So when you feel you are ready to heal, ask for the guidance you need. Then watch for the signs and the support you need, allowing your healing and transformation to start.

Remember, everything in life is just an experience to help you grow and make you stronger.

But If You Really Loved Me You Would

Have you ever played the game of always being treated the same? No matter what you do, it's never good enough from you. You work so hard to show your love, doing everything you could. Keeping your other, a perfect lover, so they would love and respect you. No matter how hard you try, they keep wanting more and more.

You think to yourself, where is their love that they seem to hide. Surely it's in there, but they never really show it. You believe that one day soon, they will tell you that they love you, or how much you mean to them. But this never happens and you miss all the signs. That they will never give you their love so you continue, loving blind. They keep their own love just for themselves. You're trapped in a cycle as though nothing will divide you. They want you to stay until the bitter end.

But it's time for you to wake up and see. That this is just a cycle called co-dependency. When you come to realise that it's time to break free, you make plans to leave. You now know you're looking for a new love. One that you know you deserve, as now you see your own self-worth. You know there is someone else just waiting, ready to love you.

You're completely unaware that the cycle will repeat until you can heal and let go. If you continue to live in the old way, you will always be stuck and never really be whole. It's a programme you see that you are conditioned to believe. When you were young, you were led to understand that this is what, real love is. No one explained that this is a pattern that you have learned, and it's called co-dependency.

So now you know what is wrong, you can start to heal yourself. Take time for you and love yourself first, this is the way to completely fix you. When you have increased your own self-worth, and can actually love yourself first, you will then see it's just a matter of time, until you meet someone new, who has the same qualities as you. You now know how to attract the most perfect match for you, who will always be independent but love just like you.

You have come to realise by now that love is all around. The secret you see is to let it flow, never controlling where it should go, or how it should be between you and another. Respect the love however it goes, and allow the process then, who knows. You may be surprised at how much love you can feel, but knowing that this time, it's definitely real.

Creating Your Life

Gently floating down the stream thinking of all the things you dream. How wonderful it is, that you can create a new life with love and happiness in it. As you imagine how it will be, you find yourself vibrating more positively. For now, you know the secret of your desire, is to keep your vibration growing higher and higher.

Planting your seeds, watching them grow. Tend to your creation, watch it flow. As it comes more to life flourishing most beautifully, following the light. I created that you say! With a loving connection, I shared each day.

You know there is nothing more you need to do, just keep remaining positive, and letting everything flow to you. You become like a magnet, attracting everything in your life. You find it's just a new way of being you in this new world as your vibrating high.

You connect with many along the way helping to shine your light in every way. To touch the hearts of all the souls you meet. Then you realise they are just another aspect of me.

Dance to Happiness

Dance your way to happiness, dance your way with joy. Finding your own beat to the music, that makes your own heart just go with the flow. Moving your body and feeling the vibes as you dance around the floor. Free all the energies that are trapped inside. As you surrender, release and let go.

Notice how you feel alive, how your feelings change with different music and different styles. As you come to life, your mood is now lifting and you're feeling happy again. You continue dancing to the music, in time with the beat. Clap your hands, stamp your feet, even singing along to your favourite songs. As you recite the words that you never seem to forget. The songs from long ago still stuck in your head.

You discover your own happiness as you continue to dance. The time passes more quickly as you continue to groove. Notice how your favourite music helps to improve your mood. Raising your vibration to the songs you love to hear. If you continue to keep this up long enough you will become a brand new version of yourself for sure.

Dark Night

There may be times when life gets tough. You're pushed to your limits and you've just had enough. The nights might be long as you try to sleep. Lying awake with all the fears you keep, churning around inside your head. You hide under the covers, not wanting to get out of bed. Trying to make sense of it all, some might say it's the dark night of the soul.

You don't want to venture outside any more. You go into hermit mode away from it all. You may seek advice from trusted friends, tarot readers, psychics or even astrologers. Hoping to find the solutions to help you through, but in reality, they never do. They may bring some relief for a while, but in all honesty, it's really down to you to fix the inside.

To do your inner work, face your fears. To accept your shadows which are buried deep within. Sometimes the shadow is really your light which you hid away from everyone since you were a child. You recall the memories of the things that you try to forget, the secrets that you kept to yourself, and never do you speak.

But once you accept your whole self and release what you need no more. You will then feel brand new and fully transformed, as a new version of you is now being born. You may be wondering how long this all takes, but your journey is unique, it's a personal thing.

The most important thing to remember as you experience this is to allow it to run its course and try not to resist. For if you try to take control, the longer it will take, causing you further heartache, pain and suffering as you try to hold onto the past. Let it go and embrace the change, knowing deep down it is for the best. The only thing to do right now is to just go with the flow and allow, let your higher self do the rest.

Don't Feed into Fear

Fear is just an illusion that likes to take hold of your mind. Fear enjoys it when you believe all the false information to keep you all in line. It continues to grow the more you believe. You're over thinking what is not real. You continue to allow fear to take hold of your life.

Your thoughts increase as you believe the lies you are told. Your imagination starts to run wild. All your logic and rational thinking start to decline. You go into a panic as you absorb the fear. Creating further beliefs, that is not true, as you listen to others who are fearful too.

Take back your power and clear your mind. Release the fear which has taken hold of you. Trust your intuition to know what is true. Don't believe all the lies that you are fed. Don't let fear get inside your head. Choose to create your own reality. Don't let it be fear-based lies created by the media and the corrupt elite.

Do You Compare Yourself to Others?

Comparing yourself to others is not a very smart thing to do. When you were young this is what you were probably taught to do. Never questioning your elders or even asking why. They programmed you so skilfully without even blinking an eye.

You may have been rebellious and tried to stand your ground. Saying you accept everyone even in the crowd. You stuck up for the weakest ones and made them your best friends. Only then to become the outsider to where people did seek revenge.

You could always see the truth in them even way back then. You could never get them to listen to you or even make amends. Trying to get them to change their ways they could never really see. That comparing one against another kept them from being free.

Embrace Your Light

Embrace your light; accept every part as you reunite. For these are all aspects of your own soul, longing to come together once more to be whole. Merging them together within your heart, knowing you will no longer ever be apart. Acceptance is usually a good place to be; soon you will discover you start to feel free. As the loves begin to grow deep down inside, you begin to stand tall with dignity and pride.

Remembering, now who you are truly meant to be, a loving co-creator, a divinely guided sovereign being.

Express Yourself

When you feel lost in your emotions just remember to breathe. Allow them to flow and release naturally. Don't try to stuff them back down inside. Express yourself, let yourself be you. Emotions are meant to flow naturally as we experience life. When we stop allowing our emotions from flowing they become stuck.

How many times have you stopped yourself from expressing your emotions? Express yourself. Be you!

Fear is an Illusion

Fear is an illusion that we are all taught. They prevent us from thriving at our skill or our art. We try to stay safe, keeping away from all harm. Following the rules and obeying all the laws. This creates more haters, more violence and more crime. We are divided by our faith and religion all of the time.

We trust in the systems that are put into place. The structures, the boundaries or for the money it makes. We follow the government, always trusting in them. But it's all just a system, which is corrupt as well.

We are now all waking up to the truth, seeing the deceit and the lies. For the elite are finally losing control, they have nowhere else to go, nowhere else to hide. Their time is nearly up for them, as we can now all see. That the fear we believed was real, is not our reality.

Fear has kept us all apart, fighting with each other. But now it's time to come together, supporting one another. We are all finally uniting now, taking back our power. We welcome in the love and light as we raise our vibration higher. We notice that our fears have gone as we all transpire.

Together now living in harmony building our new world. Following our spirituality, not the corruption we have learned.

Finding the Real You

Sometimes in life, it takes great inner strength to be you. To find the truth of whom you really are. Being caught up in the drama of life can prevent you from seeing the truth. You trust blindly as you only want to see the good in others. You want to believe that everyone shares the same values as you.

Unfortunately, we are not all the same. We learn through our experiences in life, sometimes repeating them again until we finally understand the truth. We actually choose how we want to respond to life. We have full control over our emotions, our thoughts and what we want to believe. It is really up to you to recognize this and choose how you wish to interact with life.

Always trust your intuition; your answers are within you. Listen to your heart and follow your inner guidance. Do what is right for you. Love yourself first. Believe in yourself always. But most importantly enjoy life and have fun.

Friends

Friends are more like family if the truth be told. It doesn't matter what your age is, whether you're young or old. When we resonate with them, they become more precious than gold. We treasure their friendship and the love they hold. Some only stay for a short time, to offer support and a helping hand. While others will be there for a lifetime of which you will be glad.

To share with you, all the good times and the bad, the troubles and strife, the fun and the laughter, or even tears and pain, when we experience sorrow and grief from deep within. They will always lift your spirit and help you through your day, even be your sunshine after the rain. They brighten up your day and help you get through, creating many memories from the times that they have shared with you.

They love you each day with no questions asked. Through thick and thin just like your kin. They always feel familiar to you. Then you recognise that feeling in your heart, that they are your soul family and will never be apart. You know they have shared many other life times with you. If you look a little bit closer you will see they are just another aspect of you.

Give Gratitude

Give gratitude for all the wonderful things you are blessed with every day. No matter how big or small they seem. By being grateful for everything in your life also sends out positive vibes. This allows the universe to send you more. It makes you aware of what you have already. It also changes your mind from focusing on what is negative in your life, as you will be spending your time giving gratitude for everything you do have instead.

I give thanks throughout my day. It is a conscious choice I make. But it teaches me how to be grateful for everything I have and experience.

Give a Little Smile

Give a little thought during your day. Smile at every person that comes your way. Even if you find you have nothing to say, a smile can most definitely lighten up their way. You never know what sorrows they hide, or how many tears they may have cried. A smile can brighten up their day, and help to take their cares away.

A smile that comes from your own heart, is a great way of giving, a great way to start. Smile when you're happy, smile when you're not, you will find it keeps growing until you're laughing a lot. Everyone may wonder what is making you smile, you can say it's that feeling you have deep inside.

Try it you say laughing some more, it's always with you, it's the love in your core. So remember to smile, because now you know, how much further your own loving feelings can flow. Now you know the secret I have shared with you. You can smile too as you go on your way, smiling at strangers to cheer up their day.

If you pay attention and take a closer look, you may catch a glimpse of them smiling at you. As they acknowledge your smile, you now know why. They too know the secret of the love they have inside. They lovingly share it with you as they pass you by.

Give Thanks Everyday

Each morning as I awake, I tell myself to have a nice day! Wherever I go and whatever I do, I always show my gratitude and say thank you.

It's not until you become aware and appreciate all the blessings you have will the universe respond and send you many more.

Remember to smile and share your love. Focusing on your passion you feel inside. Fill your heart with pure joy, as you feel the connection to nature and all mankind.

What you give another can make all the difference, to someone who is in need of assistance. So remember to give thanks and show gratitude, because one day you might find you need help too.

Go Within

Leave the shallow waters behind as you dive deep into you. Searching for a deeper meaning you know you once knew. It's time to journey inwards now to connect to the real you. Feeling the divine love inside, uniting all aspects of you.

Don't keep those darkest fears alive any more than you need to. Let go of the outside world that has tried to control you. Your freedom lies within you now if you go inside you will see. That everything you believe you are has already come to be.

It's time to wake up now and remember who you are. The doors of time have opened now and can't control you anymore. The deceit and lies you have been told and the stories you have been fed. Can't keep you trapped anymore or control what's in your head.

It's time to bring more light into the world so we can live in peace, not war. Having love and compassion in our hearts in which we can share once more.

Gratitude

Gratitude is a good place to start, to give thanks from within, thanks from your heart. It's the little things in life that make us who we are. When you remember this then you will go far. Help all you can along the way, unconditionally is the preferred way. It's never too late to make a start, with a helping hand or a loving thought. Shine bright as a star from morning until night, spreading love to everyone so together we can unite. Remembering it was gratitude where you did start and this loving feeling deep down in your own heart.

Growing Up

When you are young and growing up people tend to ask you what you are going to do. You dream of everything you wish to be. An astronaut, a pilot, may be someone famous on TV. I'm going to be famous when I grow up, live in a mansion, drive a fast car, have money and diamonds and all that I ask for.

But soon you notice your dream has gone, everything you ever wanted never came along. You work so hard just to make a living. Everyone around you seems to take more than they are giving. This isn't the world that I could see for me. I know this is wrong. It's all been taken from me.

But if you could only see you have all the things you will ever need. Not the material pleasures that you seek. But the love you have inside your heart. No one can ever own that part. This is the part you get to keep. When you remember I just need to be me.

Happiness Now

Are you someone who thinks that you can only be happy when you achieve your goals? That happiness can only be experienced when you have what you want.

Do you realise that you can choose to be happy now regardless of anything?

There are no conditions or limitations on happiness. Only you choose to do that. You are actually in control of when and how you choose to be happy.

So whatever you currently believe about happiness review your beliefs today. Choose to be happy now! Do anything you can to be happy today. Then make a conscious choice to keep doing whatever you are doing that is making you happy.

It can be absolutely anything as long as it makes you happy. It can even be a hobby or an interest that brings you instant happiness. Put your focus on that.

After a while, you may begin to notice how different you feel. You may notice that things are starting to slowly change in your life. Your vibration will automatically change as you focus on just being happy.

Then you can honestly say "that no matter what happens in my life...I choose to be happy!"

Happy Thoughts

Wake up to happy thoughts each and every day. Give thanks and gratitude for all the abundance you're blessed with, throughout your day. Be kind and caring to everyone you meet, greet them with a smile, treating them with love and respect. And at night before you go to sleep always say your prayers. For nothing in life is ever promised to you, not even your worries or cares.

I Feel Like

Your emotions are very powerful. They are how you respond to life. They fluctuate throughout your day, even when you find you have nothing to say. You still feel your emotions deep inside, flowing through your body as you connect them to your mind.

You may be feeling happy or maybe even sad. Sometimes you get angry and can feel really mad. You can laugh or cry at what people do or say, or how they react towards you as you go about your day.

You can feel love for someone special who means everything to you. You can even feel pain or grief when they leave you. Or maybe sometimes you feel happy and free as you're pleased to see them go and you watch them leave.

Sometimes you may be depressed or sad not knowing how you feel, just really empty and numb which goes deep down to your core. Then there is shock and trauma which can play havoc on your mind, leaving you feeling in complete fear or anxious and confused for a very long time.

But the best feelings of all are the ones that make you smile. Feel happiness and joy that gives you such a high. You can share your feelings with others too, but sometimes your empathy feels things that just aren't you.

So it's best to learn how you feel so you can express yourself openly with all you meet. Learn to understand your emotions and know what are yours, as they are a guide to know what's true and really inside of you.

In Isolation

When you're stuck in doors and climbing up the wall, you seem to get bored quickly whatever you find to do. Maybe you're scrolling through social media on your mobile phone, trying to find things to keep you entertained, the whole day through.

The T.V is on and the music is playing too, as everyone wants to do their own thing, all in one room. The dog has been walked morning, noon and night, when they hear you mention walkies they start to put up a fight. The cat is playing it safe watching your every move wondering if you will put on a lead and try to walk it too.

You give up on your diet as food is in short supply, so you ration what you have, as you are told to stay inside. You continue to watch the news which just confuses you more. You never really know what is true, it just creates more fear.

You hear how many people have died and you're hoping and praying that you will stay alive. Waiting for your turn in the vaccine queue thinking this is your only answer to help to save you. You hope that you will make it through to live another day, as you cry and weep for all the innocent people who have already passed away.

You then begin to realise just how lucky you are, as you spend precious time with the ones you love, that you have taken for granted for so long. You get to see how precious they are and feel your love grow even more.

You come to realise in the end that you got your priorities all wrong and try to make amends. When this is all over I hear you say I will live my life so differently in every way. I can now see all the blessings I have in my life; they were there this whole time, right before my eyes.

Inside Your Heart

Whenever you feel lost and you're looking where you fit in. A very good place to start is inside your very own heart. This is what connects you to your reality. It's the place to go when you're feeling all alone. This is the place that is known to you. It's the place that feels like home!

Inspire

Some of the things you're inspiring to be, healthy, strong, courageous, positive, bright, loving, caring, honest, fun, successful, beautiful, intelligent, sensitive, loyal, powerful and free.

Then you realise I'm thinking about me. I am them already. They are all inside of me!

It's All a reflection of You

Life is just a reflection of your reality. The outside is only showing you what you already believe. You may not be aware of what's in your subconscious mind. It could be a programme that has been there for quite some time.

The outside mirrors every part of you. Some you like, some you don't and some you just won't admit to. The only way to make the change is to take a look inside. To do the inner work, that can take some time.

It's all about perception and what you believe is true. It's time to expand your mind and try something new. Once you make the changes within, the outside eventually does the same. It will always show you you're reflection of what is inside of you.

This is where real change begins. You have all the power within. The more you change and understand yourself, the more new things will start to show up for you. It's your own beliefs that are keeping you stuck, your patterns and programmes, your childhood wounds.

Do your inner work, discover who you are, surrender, release and clear what isn't yours. Only keep what you know is truly you. Then all the amazing qualities you now have within will begin to reflect back at you, from outside for sure.

It All Starts With an Idea

It only takes one thought to plant a seed. Once your seed is planted, allow it time to grow. Trust that it has everything it needs. Eventually, you will see the first signs of it taking form.

Remember... Allow it to grow freely. Don't try to make it grow more quickly or try to control how it grows. This will only interfere with the natural process so please be patient. Eventually, you will be able to reap the rewards. Everything in life has a cycle. When you acknowledge this your life will flow naturally.

It's Time to Express Yourself

Express yourself in all that you say. Express yourself in a compassionate way. Be wise, be bold, be brave, and be true. Speaking of your truth you know it's time you do. Stand up and be proud, say it out loud. Never feel afraid to speak, even in a crowd. Share your loving words with the world. Tell them how life will unfold. For the new world is here. As you continue to cheer, peace is the new way to be. The earth is transforming, a new day is dawning and everyone will soon be free.

I Wonder

I wonder what goes through your mind as you sit quietly as time goes by. Do you think of things in your past or maybe remember the people you once knew. Do you remember the times gone by, all the experiences that you did try? Some losses, maybe some gains, the old and the new. Love, joy and laughter some pleasure and pain. Remembering all of the memories that made you, you.

So as you sit in your quiet space, allow this opportunity to now create, all the new things you would like in this world. This is your chance to start again, to show you the real value of life my friend. It's not the material things that define the real you but what is already inside, deep within you. The love you have is the purest thing. It's what connects you, to every living thing.

We have the chance to make things right. Open our hearts and shine our light. To teach the children who are now being born, to create a new system that's fair to all. Share our love across the world, to come together and create a new earth. Fill it with love and peace throughout all mankind, making a difference to humanity. Now is the time to come together, so we can stand united & set us all free.

Just For Today

Just for today, try to do your best.
Just for today, spread love and happiness.
For today is the day, that matters the most.
It's the now moment, which comes first.
Honour today and live it well.
Spending time on your own,
With family, or with friends,
However, you decide, to choose to spend your day.
Give thanks and gratitude, for the miracles that come your way.

Keep On Shining

We all need to shine our light. To expose the darkness that is still trying to hide. The truth is revealed the more we shine, as we transform the darkness into light.

We are all one, we are all the same, but some of us got lost along the way. This is now a time to choose, if you continue to follow the darkness you will eventually lose.

Find the love inside your heart this is where you can start. Face your shadows, embrace your fears. Address everything that needs to be healed. Accept every part of you. Your masculine, your feminine, your inner child too, then integrate them together with your higher self within you.

Love yourself for just being you. Then share your love across the land, to offer assistance whenever you can. To reach out to all in need, to all join together in unity. Spread your light wherever you go, shine so bright so that others follow. So they too can do their part to assist Gaia in creating new earth.

Keep Shining Bright

Everywhere you go transmuting all the darkness, as you continue to glow. Glow among the shadows leaving them no place to hide. Restore peace and harmony throughout the land. Love and freedom are what we want to create. Release all the suffering, pain and hate. Create a new life of joy within our hearts. Liberating humanity so together we can unite.

Kindness

Kindness is recognised by one and all. No matter your beliefs or where you come from. We can all choose to be kind each and every day. Showing true kindness in a very heartfelt way, by being kind to all that we meet, offering a smile or even a kind word, going out of our way to help someone in need.

Kindness is very much needed in this world, leading by example so that everyone can see. That being kind will always be the preferred way to be. To offer kindness should not be seen as weak, though there may be some who would take advantage if they could.

But the kindest people that you will ever meet are those that are known as the very old souls. They can never be manipulated, no matter whatever they are told. For their kindness comes from their own heart, it is a pure form of their love. Kindness is given to everyone they meet with no hidden agenda at all. Their love and kindness can light up your way and help you weather any storm.

Laugh Every Day

Remember to laugh each and every day. Laughter is the medicine to take all your worries away. A good sense of humour is definitely what you need, as you wake up to 5D at great speed. For laughter is the gift we have been given from the divine. To share a good joke or two, along with a great punch line. If you're feeling sad and blue, finding it hard to make it through. Try laughing instead, even if it's just in your head, it can make a great difference to you.

Laughter

They say that laughter is the greatest medicine of all. We can all enjoy laughter whenever we choose. It's the greatest gift we have been given. We do this naturally without even a thought. It lifts our spirit and lights up our heart.

We all respond to laughter no matter what we believe. It's the easiest thing that we can all achieve. Learning to laugh at your self is the biggest lesson of all. Not to take life too seriously even when you fall.

Laughter comes along to save the day. To lift your vibration so you may continue on your way. So if you're feeling blue, remember laughter will see you through. Laughter is the best cure for all your worries and strife. So remember to laugh throughout your day, it just might help take your worries away.

Life is a Rollercoaster

Have you ever thought awakening is like a rollercoaster?

It can be the most thrilling; intense, scariest, amazing ride of your life ever, you know, once you get on, there is no going back!

You just know you have to ride it...holding on tight...afraid to let go...You can scream all the way if you want to. You can close your eyes and pretend you're not here!

You may want to pray that you survive and hope it's all over soon. You know you have no control! You feel every emotion as you go up and down twisting and turning...It all happens so fast. Before you know it you're slowing down, you have reached the end. It's all over...You made it...You survived.

How was your experience?

100

Light Workers

When you are feeling all alone or have a longing to go home. Just remember you have a job to do and you can leave when you are through.

You're here to help raise the vibration of this planet, helping all who choose to ascend who are on it. To support mother earth as she transitions too assisting her into 5D earth to start anew.

We're heading into the fifth dimension with your help and intervention. So when you're feeling lonely inside try to connect with members of your soul family far and wide. We're all here to shine our light to offer love and to reunite.

We're making progress in every way as more and more awaken now each and every day. The darkness is failing to keep us in fear they realise they have no control for their own gain. Their time on this planet is nearly done as we raise the vibration they will soon be gone.

In the fifth dimension together we will be happy and free content living in loving harmony.

Listen to Your Heart

Listen to your heart, it is calling to you. Listen to your heart, it knows what to do. When your world seems so lonely, the people are so cruel. When you're tired of the drama and it's too much for you. Listen to your heart. It's time to go. Don't hold onto old structures, just go with the flow.

For tomorrow is coming without any doubt. Release your old patterns, just clear them out. When you do then you'll notice you're becoming happy and free. Connecting with your heart is the best thing you'll see. Collapsing all your timelines, all your parallel lives. Uniting all together your heart and mind.

Listen to your heart, as you become one. Listen to your heart, now your worries have gone. For the future is brighter where you're going you'll see. But now is the moment, the best place to be.

Love without Attachment

We may love everything while we can and cherish it and watch it grow. Love is best without attachment so we can see all the beauty that it truly holds. But if we try to hold on too tightly, eventually it will flee. As it tries to escape your suffocating claws, it will constantly try to break free. If it stays trapped for too long it will eventually wither and die. Because love is best when, it's treated as a bird with wings so it can take flight.

Love is best when it is free, allowing it to come and go. If you find it in your heart, to respect what love needs, eventually you will see that it chooses to stay and to continue to evolve and grow. You get to enjoy love at its best as it returns itself to you. Then you will eventually see that love is part of you.

Love

Love is created within the heart.
This is where it will start.
Deep, deep down these feelings will grow.
Where they end up only you will know.

Manifesting Your Desires

Gently floating down the stream, thinking of all the things you dream. How wonderful it is that you can create a happy new life with a loving soul mate, or whatever you desire. As you imagine how it will be, you find yourself vibrating more positively. For you know the secret of your desire is to keep your vibration growing higher and higher.

You know there is nothing more you need to do. Just keep remaining positive letting everything flow to you. You become like a magnet attracting everything. You find it's just like a new way of life as you manifest everything you have ever wanted for yourself.

You have learned not to give your power away or to let other people lead you astray. You know it is all about keeping a positive mind and the loving feelings which all come from within, that creates the new life for you as you continue to live in your joy all day through.

It doesn't matter what you stay focused on as long as you maintain your vibration as high as you can. This is what brings your manifestation to you it's known as the law of attraction by many of you.

Keep an open mind on how it will arrive or how it will be presented to you in good time. You don't want to limit whatever you seek as it may be something more amazing than you could ever imagine it to be. Just know it will be for your highest good and a vibrational match just for you.

My Bestest Friend

How amazing friendship can be. I remember my bestest friend when I was only three. We played together at the nursery, having so much fun.

Playing on the slide together, painting pictures and sitting together at storytime when the day was nearly done. He was my Bestest friend ever, we did everything together.

But one day a big van came and packed up all his things. He said he was moving on, and would soon be gone, as he said goodbye to me. It broke my heart as I sat and did cry, my little friend was leaving me behind and I didn't know why.

I thought it was my fault, why did he have to go. I hoped he would stay, oh how I prayed and prayed. I was so happy with my little friend, but no matter how I tried, or the tears that I cried, all I could do was watch him go.

I always remembered my first little friend. He left a lasting impression at such a young age. I never did forget his name; I still remember our friendship until this very day.

I did meet up with him again later in my life, but our friendship was not the same, as the spark had seemed to have died. I never did ask him if he still remembered me, I suppose that it was my secret about our friendship when I was three.

I never even told him how it made me feel, that on the day he left and drove away, it broke the heart in me.

My Perfect World

In my perfect world, everything is divine and I choose to live free and happy all of the time. There is no corruption or man-made laws that keep me trapped in a system with poverty or sickness, fighting, crime or wars.

In my perfect world, I have great abundance, I share what I have and have all my needs met. I'm not made homeless living in the street or living in poverty in a system controlled by the elite. In my perfect world, I know the truth of who I am. I'm a powerful creator, a part of the divine plan.

But in this world that I know now, I'm here to wake up the people and expose all I can, of the corruption that is designed to control the masses. I know the systems are not broken; they are designed to work this way. They are here to trick you into slavery and keep you trapped in a system to take your power away. The elite need your energy to keep on living, so they rely on you to keep on giving & giving.

In this world I live in now I choose to take back my power and give to the system no more. I no longer choose to live in fear of the programmes and lies or the corrupted man-made laws. I know the truth of who I am. I am a sovereign being, governed only by spiritual law.

In my perfect world, I know that I am free. I now get to live my life the way it was designed to be. I choose love, happiness and joy for all who live in this perfect world and beyond. A world of peace where we know and remember we all come from source and we are all one.

Never-Ending Story

Life is like a never-ending story. The beginning is remembered as the day you were born. You continue on your journey as the days pass you by. You remember the main events in your life, as a marking of time. A birthday, a marriage, the birth of your child or even the death of a loved one as they depart this life.

Each experience you have is like a new chapter for you. Some may be long, happy and fun, while others are short and not so sweet. It all depends on your reality on how you will react. Every experience we have in life can have a huge impact. What we think and what we do. How we learn and how we grow.

When we're successful we can move forward, taking the lessons as things we have learned. Sometimes we repeat them again in life, as we may not recognise the repeating patterns at first. We finally get it though in time, as we continue on our journey in this current life.

We believe that our end is when we die when we go onto heaven way up in the sky. But that is not the end as we know it, as life is like a never-ending story, our spirit will live on long after this life, for this is just a chapter we experience in this human body.

Plant Your Seeds

Plant your seeds, watch them grow. Tend to your creation, watch it flow. As it comes more to life, flourishing most beautifully, following the light. I created that you say! With a loving connection shared each day.

Positive Vibes

Positive vibes will keep you vibrating high, as you set your intentions to feel all happy inside. Buzzing along, feeling positive vibes with a smile on your face, which you wear with pride. People will wonder what secrets you keep, as you shine your light for everyone to see. It's no secret I hear you say it's just my positive vibes helping to brighten up my day! They keep you in the flow as you enjoy your day, helping you to express yourself in a positive way. Try it and see how it makes you feel then you can have positive vibes just like me!

Seeing Past the Illusion

When the veils begin to lift, you start to see through the fog. You can understand all the confusion. You've been having for so long. Knowing it was just an illusion. Your eyes are now open wide. You see the truth for what it is; it has no more places to hide. Now you can choose a new direction, a new way in which to go. Releasing your wounds from the past will now allow your life to flow.

Self Love

Learning to love yourself is very hard to do when you listen to everyone else's opinion of you. You take on beliefs that are not entirely true, preventing the loving connection inside of you. It's time to connect with your own heart. To love every aspect of the real you, to let go of all these outdated beliefs, that you know deep down are just not you.

Listen to your heart as it guides your way, back to loving you more, each and every day. Know that you're loveable in your own way. You don't need to be like anyone else no matter what they say. You need to be you and love yourself first, as you live your life as you are meant to do. To be a shining example for all the world to see that it's not being selfish to really love me!

Shadow and Light Unite

Embrace your shadow, embrace your light. Accept every part of you as you reunite. For these are all aspects of your own soul, longing to come together once more to become whole. Merging them together within your heart knowing you will no longer ever be apart.

Acceptance is usually a good place to start to feel free. As love begins to grow deep down inside, you begin to stand tall with dignity and pride. Remember now who you are truly meant to be a loving co-creator, a divinely guided sovereign being.

Shine Bright

Keep shining bright everywhere you go transmuting all the darkness as you continue to glow. Glow among the shadows leaving no place to hide. Restore peace and harmony throughout the land. Love and freedom are what we want to create. Release all the suffering, pain and hate. Create a new life of joy within our hearts. Liberating humanity so together we can unite.

Stand Your Ground

Don't let anything stand in your way; don't even listen to what negative people say. You just keep on moving along ready to sing your victory song!

Just remain positive as you stay on track, keep a watchful eye for haters who try to hold you back. Don't let them stop you, my friend. You know you will be a winner in the end. Stand your ground and remain strong, lead by your example and show them how it's done!

Get back into your groove, let nothing stand in your way. Being a trailblazer lighting up the way, finding others to join you in your quest, learning how to be your best.

Let love and laughter lead you on feeling good vibrations all day long. As you learn how to get your groove on remembering to keep singing and dancing to your special song.

Stepping into Your Power

When you hear the calling from deep inside, the stirring of your passion as it starts to ignite. Don't shy away from the things that you know. It's divine guidance for the path you must follow.

Listen very carefully to the truth you are told, using your discernment, being brave and being bold. Stepping into your power of which you truly are, know you can no longer hide, or try to stay small.

It's time to acknowledge the real reason you are here. To bring enlightenment to others, so they too may see. They also have a choice to make to step into their power and to start anew just like you.

Sunshine

Each morning as I wake I'm greeted by the sun. It helps me to begin my day and makes it feel like fun. When I feel the sunshine gently shining down on me, it makes me feel so happy, so loving and so free.

Sunshine is my loving friend as it provides me with vitamin D. This is very good for me as it keeps me very healthy. But remember not to play out too long as it can make you very sick. It can dehydrate you very quickly and even burn your skin.

So remember to take care as you enjoy the sun. That way you get the best of it each day as you continue to play and have fun.

Time to Wake Up

If you have been awake for some time and everyone that you meet are still asleep. They may think you're crazy or going slightly mad for the things you say you believe or what you may say you know. They probably don't know what to say, or how to interact with you. They may just stare at you or try to move away.

The funny thing though that they may not yet know is that they will finally see your reality as they wake up, they will discover that you knew all along, that it was them who actually got it wrong. They will see they have been kept in the dark about who they really are, living in an illusion in the 3d reality.

They will now come to see you have been wide awake all this time, watching them all just toeing the line. Playing out their drama each and every day caught up in their own illusions of the stories that they create. All this time just playing along until they finally wake up to the truth.

They will then remember who they really are as they wake to their new reality and recall even more. Maybe then they will smile to themselves as they too will now see. That they now believe the things you do and say, they know they are all really true, and if they now speak their truth they will also be called crazy just like you.

The Ego

The human ego is big and bold. It never likes to be told what to do or where to go. It can rule you when it takes hold.

It likes to control everything you do. It thinks it is doing what is best for you, keeping you safe from any harm, saving you from danger or doing something wrong. It remembers everything you say. It's very clever that way.

Gaining power, more and more, it's afraid of dying, of becoming no more. When you realise it's not serving you well. Its intentions are all in a mess. From all the things that you have learned which are conditioned in your mind. The programmes are all wrong which it still tries to hide.

It lets you think that you have won. If you're aware of how it has become. It then pretends it has died, but you know it is only really trying to hide. The only way to change its view is by making it a friendly part of you. To listen to it quietly in the back of your mind then thanking it for being there saying that's so very kind.

The Flow of Life

How wonderful life is when you're in the flow. All dilemma's and dramas are a no go. You leave all the worry and fear behind. Your experiences are all now considered divine, as your intuition keeps things in perfect time.

Everything now happens as it should. You knew deep down that it always would. As you trust and surrender to this thing called life. All your cares and worries are blessed by the light. Receive love each and every day keeping things flowing in every way.

You cherish each moment living in the now. For tomorrow is the future which you know somehow, will be just as perfect as it has been today. It hasn't been written yet as it's too far away. But remember your wishes and your dreams too. So when you get in the flow they can all come to you.

Living in the flow of life brings love and laughter. Joy and happiness too, if that is what you are after. There may be times when you feel alone or feel you can't go on. This will pass sure enough when you remember we are all one. Remember this is just a process that we all choose to do. Raise your consciousness, bringing complete awareness to you.

The New Earth is here

There is a different kind of silence in the world today. Everyone is stuck indoors not allowed out to play. Only the animals, the birds and the bees continue their day. The plants and flowers, bushes and trees all continue to grow in the cycle of life. They respect Mother Nature each and every day, they try to get our attention to the mess mankind creates. The pollution to the environment is killing off our world. It's time to stop and put it right before it gets too late. It's time to take a new approach if we want to survive and co-create.

Mother earth won't wait forever for us to get it right. She is now transcending, creating new earth. Taking only those who have chosen to ascend with her, who are awake and value her world. The time has come to make your choice during this great divide.

Do you choose to create new earth or do you stay behind? The time has come to wake up to the truth, to raise your vibration high. For those who choose to remain in the dense energy will have no choice but to stay right here where they are and eventually die. The darkness won't be permitted into the new earth to continue with their war, to continue to corrupt and keep you all as slaves with their dark agenda and lies.

The masses are now awakening to the truth of who they truly are. How they have given their power away and been controlled for far too long. It is time to stand up to the system that is corrupt and controlling you by fear. The way to reclaim your power is through your very own heart. Your heart has always known the truth that it holds pure consciousness inside. This is your protection to keep you safe and connect you to the divine.

The Weather

Does the weather influence your day? Do you cancel your plans or carry on anyway? Does the weather make you feel blue or make you feel happy and all brand new?

It's funny how the weather can dictate your day. Staying at home or going out to play. As the seasons come and go, autumn, winter, summer and spring. The sun, the snow, the wind and the rain all have an impact as you go about your day.

We listen to the weather report so we can plan our day ahead but then we find they got it wrong and it's the opposite of what they said.

Expect some rain, and fog patches too, some snow on the hills, maybe some hailstone in the afternoon, mixed up with sunshine around noon. The gales force winds will be quite a storm, if you're lucky enough it won't be for long. Brace yourself for the hurricane that is surely on its way, if you're lucky enough they will name it after you. It will be minus ten during the night so wrap up warm until daylight.

We think that just about sums up the weather they say! We have mentioned every aspect just in case. But be prepared for the worst! This is the final thing said by the weather host, as they tell you to enjoy the weather, have a nice day, hope it is good whatever.

Trust Your Vibes

When you question what you see. Wondering if this is your reality. Never doubt yourself in any way. Trying to accept what others may have to say. For that may only be their truth, their reality. Making you question everything, including your sanity. Listen to your intuition and you will find your inner guidance is never blind.

You may find the truth you seek is never right for them. Although they may keep on trying to convince you that it is also their truth as well. They only want you to stay the same, to stop you from moving on. You realise you don't fit in anymore, but they try to tell you you're wrong. But with a little practice, you will come to know. Your vibes are always true to you no matter where you go.

So never change yourself just to fit in with them. Follow your own truth so you will never be misguided again. When you choose to just be you and trust in your vibes. You will never question your truth, be misled or even deceived. You will see the truth for what it's is and choose your path. Trusting your inner guidance will always have your back.

Wake Up World

You may be feeling lost through all of this confusion. Is what you're experiencing real or just an illusion. Your mind is losing all control. You can't seem to make sense of what you're told. You're doing the best you can, trying to get through another day. Hoping and praying that this will just all go away. Life as you knew it is no longer the same. You now see the changes happening each day.

Please don't give up hope whatever you do. Staying strong and remaining focused will help you get through. For when this is over you will clearly see that everyone will want to build a new reality. New times are coming in the days ahead, but for now, remain calm and stay out of your head. Live in the moment, just focus on today. Attending to what needs to be done in the now, not further away. Looking to the future will only create more fear.

So if you want to help you then start living day by day. This is how life was meant to be, not stuck in some rat race. Take the time to get to know the real you, your friends and your family, who all love you. Decide what is important in your life. Not working for money, allowing your health to decline. Saving every day for your future plan, when all that matters is the here and now. Live each moment with happiness and joy, unite with your loved ones and try to remain calm.

We will soon see the new earth which is now really needed. So remember stay strong and do what you can. Allow the universe to continue with the master plan. For soon enough you will see a new beginning on earth in a whole new reality.

What's Your Label?

When you are born you are given a name. It is who you will be known as in this life. That's okay with me you say as you probably like that name anyway. As you grow up during your childhood you just fit in like you know you should. You are just who you are and identify yourself by the name you were given at birth.

The trouble with the labels only seems to start when you try to identify with who you are. You're told you're an individual who needs to be labelled as such. There are so many labels in this world. You try to pick the things that identify you but all they do is put you in a box, separating you more and more from everybody else. There are so many labels for every aspect of your life which include your religion, culture, colour and gender, even your sexuality type.

So the labels continue throughout your life as you grow up, maybe you get married to a husband or a wife. You train in a profession to gain further status adding more labels to your identity. Your sexuality is another issue trying to decide if your heterosexual, gay, lesbian, transgender or bi, not forgetting the Q if you just think you're queer. Just to add to the confusion as you try to fit in. You wonder what your labels are and where you should begin. The list becomes endless and you become more confused. You wish you were a child again with only just your name that you use. Because life was so much simpler back then and everyone was all the same.

So as for me as time goes by, I've had so many labels now which is no surprise. I realise I don't want any of them anymore because that is not who I am...I am me with just my given name, that I will accept so people can recognise me by my name. But all the rest I completely reject as they are not who I am. I am not a label, I am not a type, I don't even have to present my profession to the world, my gender, my religion or my sexuality type, my culture or colour shouldn't even make a difference. I don't want to be stereotyped anymore or put into a box.

I am what I am and that I am proud to be me. There are no more boxes for you to put me in. I am not separate from everyone else. I am part of the collective consciousness. I do know that we all come from the same source as we are all one. We are part of our creator also known as god.

What is Love?

Love is a high vibrational thing. It's pure energy, which can be felt from within. It can never be owned, bought or sold. It lives completely freely among young and old.

It touches the hearts of each and every soul. It has the power to turn envy into gold. When you look outside yourself to find the love you seek. You may just be lucky enough to catch a glimpse or a peek. Love flows freely between each thing. It shares that warm fuzzy feeling that you feel from within.

It can make you laugh, it can make you smile, and it can even make you cry. It even has the ability to make you feel so high. It can make you feel all fluffy and light like your floating on a cloud.

If you're feeling sad and blue, or need a hug to help you through, then love can help you much indeed, to pick you up in your hour of need. Never hold on tight to the love you feel, as it needs to keep flowing, it needs to be free.

It will always be there deep in your heart, growing ever stronger, never to part. Always trust the love inside, it's your forever friend, it's your loving guide.

We All Have Beliefs

We all have beliefs; it's a part of who we are. They form our reality to define what we live our life for. Some can be helpful for a while, but when they're not we accept them anyway, & remain in denial.

We don't like change so we bury our truth. Instead, we search for meaning outside our self, looking for answers we can say is true. To cover up what we really feel, because society doesn't allow you to be you.

We follow the crowd thinking they are smart; you question why you don't feel the same as it doesn't resonate with your heart. It becomes really obvious that you don't fit in, as we inherit many more beliefs from family & friends.

You realise this brings no comfort on your path, you're not here to live like them, you're here to be free, to live your own life. To remove all limitations you were led to believe, to discover the truth of who you are.

You need to release these lies you have been fed for so long. When you discover the answers you seek, are all inside your heart. Then you can say I believe in me! I am who I am & I create my own reality.

Wishes and Dreams

Everyone has wishes...
Everyone has dreams...
Everyone has desires...

Do you know these can all be possible when you believe? They can!

Release your limiting beliefs.
Anything is possible.
If you think it, then you can have it.
It is only your beliefs that say you can't
Say yes to life.
Live your best life yet.
It's ready when you are
Just say...
Yes!

When Fear Keeps You Stuck

We all have times in our life when we outgrow the things we love. We dream about the changes we will make, about all the new things we are going to create. But the fear pops up inside our head and reminds us not to get too far ahead.

Fear lets us know that we need to stay in line, don't rock the boat or make changes to your life. Fear tells you to continue with what you already know. It doesn't want you to believe that you can go. You can choose whatever you wish but fear hopes you don't discover the truth, as it feeds off your energy & never wants you to change.

It makes you believe that you are stuck, that change only comes from pure luck. It likes to be in control of you all of the time, keeping you in check making you toe the line.

But now you know the truth about fear, the time has come to find the courage to break free. Break past the fear that has been controlling you, a better life awaits you if you do.

Fear will never regain control of your life as you break free it knows that you have won. This is the secret fear has been keeping from you, to stop you from imagining a better life for you, with all you desire to create in this world, full of love and compassion, not with fear and hate.

You Are Beautiful

All the love & beauty we hold inside is just bursting out to be shared far and wide. It's time to show the world who you truly are, shine your light bright, like a guiding star. The children need us now to show them the way. To be strong, loving and supporting in each & every way. They are our future of this new world, which we are all creating if the truth is told. Open your hearts, let us all now see, singing and dancing, feeling happy and free. Together we are creating life's new tapestry.

You Are Loved

When you feel like life is getting you down. You feel you're alone, even in a crowd. People seem too busy living their own life, to stop to say hello even once in a while. You hide away all alone pretending you're okay. You eventually give up on people as you feel that they don't care. You feel they judge you for who you are, or how you live your life. They're quick to point out the things you do wrong or try to control your life.

No one knows the truth of who you really are. They have never walked in your shoes nor have a clue about your life. They have no idea when they see you smile or how low you feel. You wear your mask so well; others never know just how unhappy in life you are. They have no idea of how you're feeling or what you are going through. People get wrapped up in their busy world so they never really notice you.

Unfortunately in life, many feel the same way. It is something that is quickly forgotten about until it is highlighted again. Many people take their own lives to free themselves from the pain. They don't know how to reach out to others or even ask for help. They think the solution to best help themselves is to bring their life to an end.

This world can be such a lonely place and people can be really cruel. Words cut very deeply and leave a lasting wound. Words can never be unspoken or taken back once said, so remember to speak kindly with love and respect. Things can get better with the right support and help, you will be happy again, in time you will mend. You are always loved by many in this world even when you don't think so.

For all of you reading this I hope the message is clear "you are loved" no matter what you think, don't let fear stop you, trust all will be well, take that step forward and reach out for help. You make a difference in this world just by being you.

Part 3 - Quotes

Accept All Aspects

Accept all aspects of yourself to become the best version of you.

Allow the Flow

Life is only a struggle if you choose to make it one. When you can allow life to flow as it is intended to do, you can face things head-on at the right moment. You may not like all the experiences you have in life, but by allowing life to flow life becomes much easier to accept.

Awake

You know you are awake when the sun shines inside of you every day as you follow your bliss.

Awakened

When you are awake and people still try to control you. Now that's funny!

Baggage

If you feel your life is a constant uphill struggle, then maybe it's time to let go of your baggage. Release all that no longer serves your highest good. Let go of outdated patterns & beliefs. Become the best version of you.

Believe in You

Sometimes it takes great inner strength to be you. Walk your own path. Stand alone in your truth. Be true to yourself. Face your fears. Keep going. Believe in you!

Be a Rebel

Be a rebel; break from your usual routine. Try something new, something different, embrace change. You may just discover something new about yourself! And like it.

Breakthrough the Veil

When you break through the veil you finally find the truth of what you have been seeking all along.

Break Free

Break free from your limiting beliefs.

Change Your Perception

When you change your perception, you allow your consciousness to expand; therefore it is inevitable that your life must change to allow for your new beliefs.

Co-dependency

Transform your life.

Break free from co-dependency.

Love yourself first.

Current Blocks

When you are ready to recognize the current blocks in your life, then you can find the solution.

Discernment

Have the ability to use your own Judgment.

This is essential guidance during the awakening process.

To be able to determine your own perception of what you consider good or bad.

Divine

Know your own worth,

Know your own mind,

Know your own truth,

Know you are divine.

Divine Timing

All will be revealed in divine timing.

Meaning...

When you become a vibrational match you can have what you desire.

Drama

Do you smile when you are aware of the current drama trying to play out in your life and you choose not to play!

Empower You

Empowering you to become the best version of you!

Empowering You

Never make excuses for who you are! Never let anyone put your light out. Stand tall and be proud. Speak your truth always.

Everything Must Go

When you compare your awakening process to a closing down sale...Everything must go!

Everything Starts with You

Everything Starts with You.

Everything Ends with You.

It's what you do in between that make all the difference in your life.

Failure

There is no such thing as a failure! Some things in life just take a few attempts to make them perfect.

Fairytale

When you realise nobody is coming to save you. When you realise you are the brave knight. When you realise you have the key to free yourself from the tower. Once upon a time, you wake up and live happily ever after.

Follow Your Bliss

When you start to see your way forward you know you are on the right path. Listen to your heart. Follow your bliss.

Follow Your Heart

Whenever you are in doubt always follow your heart.

Free Yourself

Take every opportunity when you recognise...

The patterns, the programmes, the conditioning,

Take responsibility for yourself...

Acknowledge, surrender, release

Repeat

Make it easy on you!

Let go

Set yourself free.

Future

The future is bright...The future is you.

Future is waiting

Step into your Future. It is ready and waiting for you.

Gold

All that glitters is not gold don't be fooled by what you are told.

Go with the Flow

Isn't life amazing when you go with the flow?

Allow your day to unfold naturally.

You may be surprised at how it turns out.

Greatest Strengths

Isn't it amazing when you realise that your weaknesses are actually your greatest strengths.

Happiness Now

True happiness is enjoying everything you do now in every moment. Not just thinking about how things might be in the future!

Happy Now

You don't need things, people or circumstances in your life to change before you can be happy. Choose to be happy now. It is a state of mind. You are in control of your thoughts. Have a wonderful day and be happy.

Heal Your Heart

When you take the time to heal your heart it allows you to open up to new love.

Heart

See how amazing your life can be when you put your heart into everything you do.

How Amazing You Are

Have you ever stopped to think how amazing you are just by being you? Give yourself permission today to really be you. You never know you might actually like it.

Highest Good

If everything around you seems confusing right now. Know that all will eventually become clear to you! Trust and allow the process. You are releasing all that is no longer serving your highest good.

Inspire You

If you find someone in life that inspires you pay attention. If you find someone in life who puts you down or tries to block your path. Walk away.

Intuition

Isn't it amazing how we need to scientifically prove things are good or bad for us but our intuition has always known.

Invest in You

You need to invest in all aspects of your mind, body and spirit if you wish to become the best version of you. Make that choice today. Love yourself first. You are worth the effort. Everything starts with you!

Leap of Faith

When you finally find the courage to take a leap of faith, trust that all will become clear as you follow your heart.

Let Your Life Flow

Let it be...Let it go...There will be an answer when you trust and let your life flow.

Like Attracts Like

"Like attracts like" If you don't like what you are experiencing in your life then change you. Your outside world is a reflection of you. Do you like what you see? If not then make the changes within you. Change your perception then your perception has to change you.

Love Yourself First

The most important relationship you can have in your life is with you!

Life is a Journey

Slow down! Life is all about the journey, not the destination.

Limits

The only limits you have in your life are those you set yourself.

Love

Love is created within the heart.

This is where it will start.

Deep, deep down these feelings will grow.

Where they end up only you will know.

Love You

It's okay to love you.

Love Yourself First

Sometimes the only thing in life is to choose you.

Love yourself first!

Loving Thoughts

Keep sending out loving thoughts every day.
What you send out always comes back to you.

Make that Change

Make that change now. No excuses, no ifs, no buts, no maybes, or I will when, as soon as, I know I should...Don't think...Just act. Choose to do it now... Say yes. Just do it. The time is now.

Miracles

Miracles can happen when you let go.

New Chapter

How excited do you feel when you're so ready to start a new chapter in your life? You feel it coming and you're waiting for the door to open.

Never-Ending Story

Life is a never-ending story.

It is only the chapters that changed.

Perception

When you change your perception... You allow your consciousness to expand. Therefore it is inevitable your life must change to allow for your new beliefs.

Perfect

There is no such thing as failure!

Some things in life just take a few attempts to make them perfect.

Progress

Isn't life amazing when you realise how much progress you have made in your life with all those baby steps you were brave enough to take, and then you smile to yourself.

Put Your Light On

Isn't it funny when you are stumbling around in the dark looking for something and then suddenly it dawns on you to just put the light on! Life is like that sometimes, don't you think?

We just need to remember to put our light on.

Real Change

Real change only comes from within.

Real You

Never ever be frightened to show the world the real you.

Stand up be proud of who you are always.

Remain Open

Your prayers are always heard...

Just remain open to how they are answered.

Remember

Do you ever get that feeling when you are learning something new? That at the same time, it just feels like you are just remembering it's something you already know!

Seeing is Believing

Seeing... is believing

Believing... is seeing

But which one happens first?

Shades of Grey

Not everything in life is as it first seems. Open your mind to all possibilities. See all the shades of grey.

Share Your Gifts

When you feel inspired to share your gifts with the world, be brave. Step out of the closet; you will be so glad when you do. You get the opportunity to meet more inspirational people just like you.

Share a Thought

If you can share a thought, a moment, or a smile with whomever you interact with during your day. It may be just what the person needs to help them get through another day. For each person that comes your way is never a coincidence, they do say divine timing is often at play guiding you gently throughout your day.

Slow Down

Slow down! Enjoy every moment...Yesterday has gone...Tomorrow has not yet arrived...Now is here...Now is here...Now is here...

Smiling on the Inside

When you're smiling on the inside everyone can see it on the outside.

Songs

Do you find yourself laughing when you hear a song stuck on replay in your head, especially when you're trying to sleep? You can't help but smile to yourself as it makes complete sense to your current situation.

What's your song? What is it saying to you? I wonder.

Strengths

Isn't it amazing when you realize your weaknesses are actually your greatest strengths.

Stand Up... Be Proud

Never ever be frightened to show the world the real you! Stand up...Be proud of who you are always.

Stand Out From the Crowd

Make sure you stand out from the crowd...

Be You!

Stay on Your Path

Stay on your path...

Don't allow fear to change your direction.

Solitude

Spending time in solitude gives you time to reflect on your journey. Go within to find your true path.

Succeed

If you don't succeed at first!

Never give up.

Keep trying.

Supporter

The biggest supporter you have in your life is actually you! You are always there for you. No matter what! Be kind to you. Love yourself first.

Thoughts

Your thoughts create your reality.

Time for Me

Don't allow anyone to stop you from enjoying the things in life you love.

Triggered

If someone triggers you, be happy and smile. They have actually done you a favour to help you release your trauma from deep inside.

True

Always be true to you. Live in the moment.

True Potential

Unlock your true potential...

Trust in the moment

When you question yourself or have doubts. Know that everything in life is happening at the right moment as it is supposed to. Have faith that everything will work out okay. Trust in the process. But most of all, always remember to have a great day.

Trust Your Journey

Sometimes you may think you are stuck or question your path. But always trust in the journey.

Trust the Universe

Who, what, where, when, how

Does it really matter?

Trust in the Universe.

The Universe knows best!

Allow. Go with the flow. Let it be.

Unknown

Embrace the unknown. You may be surprised at what you might find.

Validation

When you seek validation from others,

When you follow guidance outside of yourself,

Always question if it resonates with who you truly are.

Wake Up

Please don't give up hope whatever you do. Staying strong and remaining focused will help you get through. Unite with your loved ones, your family and friends. Reach out to strangers who may also need help. It is time to wake up! The future is now. Remember we are all one.

Walk Your Talk.

Walk your Talk...Your Talk! Lead by Example...Your Example! Want Change... You Change! Make a Difference... Be the Difference! Want Power... You are the Power! Everything is created inside of you! If you think it...You can have it. There are NO Limits!

Within You

When you realise that everything you will ever need in life actually starts from within you!

Wishes Become Your Reality

May all of your wishes, become your reality.

You Are Amazing

Have you ever stopped to think?

How amazing you are!

Just by simply being you.

Give yourself permission today to really be you!

You never know.

You might actually like it.

You Are Never Stuck.

You are never stuck! It's just an illusion.

When you decide to get out of your own way,

And surrender miracles can happen!

Opportunities arrive. New adventures begin.

Possibilities are endless. There are no limits!

You Choose

Nothing in life is a mistake. Happens by chance, a coincidence, good or bad, right or wrong or however else you wish to describe it. Everything you experience in life was already chosen by you.

You just don't remember

You're not broken

You're not broken. You're just you. You're only different because of what you have been through. Everything in life is just an experience to help you grow and make you stronger.

Conclusion

This brings me to the end of this book. I hope that you will take from this all that resonates with you in your current reality with an understanding that you may consciously or subconsciously recall this information as you become more awake and aware of your journey and awakening process. You may find that this book will have a deeper meaning for you as you awaken further and you may also find it a helpful guide to read when guided by your intuition as and when you feel you need further assistance or guidance.

On a personal note, I would like to leave you with a final thought about what I have personally learned and discovered about this thing called life so far on my journey in this lifetime.

Life is all about believing in you, having trust in the universe. Needing to let go of the control you think you have, learning to relax and just to go with the current flow, allowing life to unfold naturally. Responding to the opportunities you are presented with as they appear on your path. Take action only when it feels right to you. Going your way in life and walking your path. Experiencing pure joy, happiness and bliss as you share your love with the world and all the people around you that you have the opportunity to interact with each day. Being an example to others and most of all just being your authentic self living in the now.

The final words I would like to leave you with are "Keep Going"

When you are told you can never achieve your dreams. Keep going... When you are told it will never happen. Keep going... Always believe in you. That is all that matters. Never give up on your dreams. Keep going...Follow your passion. Stay motivated. You will succeed. Feel it. Know it. See it. If you think it, you can create it.

About the Author

Laura had her first awakening in 2002. Laura recalls always having a deep knowing that she had something important to do but did not know quite what it was at that time. Laura continued on her own spiritual journey through many life challenges while also working through releasing all programming and conditioning she had held since childhood. In 2006 Laura trained in hypnotherapy; counselling and psychotherapy which led her to further develop her psychic intuitive abilities. This is when she opened up to begin her channelling with the council of twelve and began her creative writing.

Laura developed a passion for crystals and continued on her own personal healing journey. She realized to bring complete balance into her life she needed to address all aspects of her physical, emotional, mental and spiritual well being. This is when she began her training as a crystal therapist. Laura specializes in distance crystal therapy and has incorporated her intuitive abilities within her therapies and sessions to further enhance them. She is able to offer insight and solutions to various issues or situations within your life. Laura offers a unique service helping you gain understanding, supporting and advising you to bring resolution quickly and as smoothly as possible while assisting you during your awakening process.

Author/Blogger, Psychic, Intuitive Empath, Channel, Crystal Therapist, Energy Healer and Spiritual Teacher.

Empowering you to live your best life!
www.crystalauratherapies.co.uk

CrystalAura Blog
Crystal therapies
One-to-One Sessions

Other books by Laura Dent
The New Earth Energy "The Council of Twelve"

Printed in Great Britain
by Amazon